Tax Subsidies and Housing Investment

This book was made possible
through a research grant with the
Economic Development Council
of New York City, Inc.

Tax Subsidies and Housing Investment

A Fiscal Cost-Benefit Analysis

George Sternlieb

Elizabeth Roistacher   James W. Hughes

THE CENTER FOR URBAN POLICY RESEARCH
RUTGERS—THE STATE UNIVERSITY OF NEW JERSEY
BUILDING 4051—KILMER CAMPUS
NEW BRUNSWICK, NEW JERSEY 08903

771675

Cover design by Francis G. Mullen
Published in the United States of America
by the Center for Urban Policy Research,
New Brunswick, New Jersey 08903

Library of Congress Cataloging in Publication Data

Sternlieb, George.

  Tax subsidies and housing investment.

  1. Taxation, Exemption from—New York (City)—Cost effectiveness. 2. Revenue—New York (City). 3. Housing—New York (City)—Finance—Cost effectiveness. I. Roistacher, Elizabeth, joint author. II. Hughes, James W., joint author. III. Rutgers University, New Brunswick, N. J. Center for Urban Policy Research. IV. Title.

HJ9289.N46S75   336.2   76-44476

ISBN 0-88285-037-7

Contents

Contents

Exhibits

Exhibits

Preface

New York City has historically served as the prototype of general governmental intervention into the private housing market. It has also been at the leading edge of specific public actions which attempt to stimulate the production of low- and middle-income housing through various tax subsidy mechanisms. By foregoing or reducing property tax payments, the city has attempted to alter housing's operating balance sheet, thereby enhancing the investment potential to private developers while lessening pressure on the spiraling rents offered to the housing consumer. Many of these efforts have been undertaken with little in the way of detailed cost-benefit analysis. It is the objective of this study to begin to rectify this situation.

The task specified by the Economic Development Council of New York City, Inc. was to establish a conceptual framework to evaluate the costs and revenues engendered by tax subsidy programs, and to formulate an operational quantitative model to analyze the effects of several specific stimulatory mechanisms. The results presented herein have substantial policy and methodological implications, not only for New York City but for all jurisdictions which have or are considering similar program measures. In addition, we believe that the overall approach and its technical components provide an initial foundation for more rigorous quantitative analyses of public policy alternatives. In an era of emerging resource scarcity, planners and policymakers must include the quantitative delineation of costs and benefits in the traditional decisionmaking matrix. This effort hopefully contributes to that end.

We would like to acknowledge the aid and assistance secured during this study not only from our colleagues at the Center for Urban Policy Research but also from the officials of New York City who readily gave their time and assistance in establishing the data resources which underpin the analysis. The Economic Development Council provided us complete freedom in our study approach, recommendations, and presentation. In the editorial arena, Ken Roberts and Barry Jones must be credited with exceptional efforts.

Needless to say, the errors that remain are those of the authors.

G.S
E.A.R.
J.W.H.

Chapter 1

An Overview

Introduction

The provision for tax subsidies to stimulate housing construction and rehabilitation is a mechanism that has not received detailed economic analysis commensurate with the scale of activity. In part this is a result of the enormous political potency that housing improvement has held in cities such as New York. The temptation to use "off the balance sheet" financing to support housing has been overwhelming. The feeling that taxes foregone (abatements and/or exemptions) are not the equivalent of out-of-pocket dollars expended has permitted a somewhat casual approach regarding the fiscal impact of such stimulative mechanisms. For many years, housing has been not only a "good" thing but, in the opinion of most New Yorkers, so desperately needed as to overwhelm those who raise issues concerning the city's fiscal competence to support it. What are the economic realities?

Our stress in the following study is on the fiscal cost-benefit elements attached to two major programs. One, the 421 program, permits tax exemption for new construction; the other, the J51 program, provides tax subsidies for rehabilitation (actual tax abatements) as well as exemptions. Our stress, again, is on the fiscal impact; i.e., the specific out-of-pocket dollars expended (costs) versus those received by the municipal fisc (revenues) as a function of the programs in question. It is only after such an analysis that the programs can be placed within the range of alternative mechanisms for maintaining and revitalizing the city.

For a long time New Yorkers have indulged in the luxury of adopting programs that are "good." Only within the last several years has there evolved a general comprehension that while many things are "good," some produce more for equivalent expenditures than others and that, given the scarcity of resources, social programs must be viewed within a cost-benefit framework. Only when this latter element is quantified can the relative desirability and payoffs of competing programs be weighed. While the dollars-and-cents cost of any program may not in and of itself determine the total value, certainly it is essential in determining an order of priority. The fiscal realities of New York demand quantitative inputs.

The scale of the programs addressed here is very large. Each involves many millions of dollars in foregone tax revenues. What does the city secure for this? Despite the growing programs, there has been relatively little analysis of what the city secures for those dollars. Particularly lacking, as will be shown in more detail later, is the quantification of key variables: How much of the activity nominally engendered by the housing subsidy programs would have taken place in their absence? How many of the tenants who occupy the facilities, either newly constructed or rehabilitated with tax aid, are newcomers to the city? How many are people who would otherwise have left the city? Are we simply playing "musical chairs" by moving the same tenantry from unsubsidized to subsidized facilities? It is very difficult indeed within the tenor of our times to criticize programs that yield improved housing conditions. But how much of the subsidies involved are redundant? Basically, what is the cost of the *net* additions to the city's housing supply? Even these questions, difficult as they are to answer, relate only to the *immediacies* of the buildings and their tenants. What are the *spillover* effects on the city's retailing? On its labor pool? On its secondary real estate values?

The work presented here attempts to draw together what data are available in order to provide a preliminary guide to the municipal decisionmaker. Clearly, much more work remains to be done before definitive answers can be given to these crucial questions. *Economics is many things—not least of which the allocation of scarce resources. We must place these two major housing tax subsidy programs on a scale that will give some measure of their potency versus their costs.*

Summary of Findings

By granting tax abatements and/or exemptions, the J51 program and the 421 program stimulate the rehabilitation of existing structures and new construction of multiple dwellings. Critics of these programs maintain that the programs subsidize New York City's upper- and middle-income households and that much of the improvement in the housing stock would have taken place in the absence of tax subsidies.

The analyses presented here indicate, however, that the initial subsidy to higher-income households and to developers may eventually generate a surplus of benefits over costs. This assumes that the projects would not have been undertaken in the absence of subsidy and that a significant portion is occupied by households who would not otherwise have resided in New York City. In this instance, the city obtains revenue from additional taxes on the nonexempt portion of increased assessed value and on expired exemptions, as well as from the generation of sales, income, and property taxes through construction spending and by households that would not otherwise have resided in the city. In addition, the spending streams from these sources ultimately are translated into increased employment, income, and spending, which in turn generate multiplied tax revenue for the city.

A quantitative model of the 421 program is constructed to estimate its net fiscal impact under alternative sets of assumptions about the stimulative effect of the program on new construction and on attracting or keeping households that would otherwise locate outside the city. Under a reasonable set of assumptions about program impact, it is found that the program generates positive revenues for the city when multiplier effects as well as more direct effects are taken into account. The present discounted value, which we establish as the net fiscal impact of the program, is $985 per unit. If multiplier effects are omitted from the analysis, however, the program incurs a net cost with a present discounted value of $746 per unit.

To obtain these final results, we determined the following set of fiscal impacts:

1. Real estate taxes foregone or created due to partial tax exemption
2. Generation of tax revenues through induced construction spending [1]
3. Generation of tax revenues through multiplier effects of induced construction spending
4. Net injection of sales and income taxes by induced residents [2]
5. Generation of tax revenues through multiplier effects of net spending by induced residents
6. Generation of real property taxes through expansion of commercial space due to spending by induced residents
7. Estimation of the per capita cost of common municipal services

Each of the specific impacts has been calculated for the twenty-five year period 1975 through 1999 and then discounted back to its present value. The present values (net fiscal impact) are then aggregated in various combinations to establish the overall fiscal impact of the 421 program under different sets of assumptions. The alternative determinations of overall impact are based on five different possible situations:

Case 1: The unit would have been built in the absence of tax exemption benefits.

Case 2: The unit would not have been built in the absence of tax exemption benefits, and the occupying tenant still would have resided *within* the city.

Case 3a: The unit would not have been built in the absence of tax exemption benefits, and the occupying tenant would then have resided *outside* the city although employed within the city. No additional commercial space would be generated and no additional cost of municipal services would be required.

Case 3b: The same as Case 3a *except* that commercial space would be generated and municipal service costs would be incurred as a result of household expansion and commercial expansion.

Case 3c: The same as Case 3b *except* that multiplier effects from construction spending and from spending of induced residents are added to the analysis.

The final results are as follows:

			CASE		
FISCAL EFFECTS	1	2	3a	3b	3c
Real Estate Taxes Foregone	−$9,010				
Real Estate Taxes Created		$16,596	$16,596	$16,596	$16,596
Net Sales and Income Tax Injection from Induced Construction		303	303	303	303
Net Sales and Income Tax Injection from Induced Residents			10,442	10,442	10,442
Real Estate Taxes on Expanded Commercial Space				2,368	2,368
Added per Household Cost of Common Municipal Services				−15,684	−15,684
Multiplier Effects of Induced Construction					1,484
Multiplier Effects of Induced Resident's Spending					14,252
Per Unit Net Fiscal Impact (present discounted value)	−$9,010	$16,899	$27,341	$14,025	$29,761

We then make assumptions about the probabilities of the pattern of distribution of units across these five cases, enabling us to suggest the most likely final impact given a large number of units. We conclude that under the most reasonable assumptions about the impact of the 421 program, taking the indirect multiplier effects of spending induced by the program into account, the benefits of the program actually exceed its costs. The initial subsidies in the form of property taxes foregone are eventually counterbalanced by the stimulation of the city's economy and by the generation of tax revenues from units that would not have been built in the absence of the program.

These conclusions do not take into account fiscal effects created if the program is part of a broad mix of programs and policies directed at revitalizing the city's economy. In this broader context, the program is likely to have even greater stimulative effects and revenue generation for the city.

The J51 program provides deeper subsidies relative to costs than does the 421 program. While its costs to the city are relatively high in terms of foregone property taxes, this program is likely to have greater power in stimulating projects which would not have been undertaken in the absence of subsidy. Nevertheless, because of the high rate of subsidy and the lower likelihood that this program will attract tenants who would not otherwise reside in the city, it seems that J51 is less likely than 421 to pay back its initial subsidy. (No complete quantitative estimate of the impact of the J51 program has been undertaken.)

Subsidies and Housing

Why does New York City require such tax subsidies and abatements in order to secure new construction and rehabilitation? Is it because overwhelming levels of property assessment and disproportionate shares of rents must go to pay taxes? Certainly the very inequities of city assessment procedures and the sheer scale of the tax burden within the city impose some level of stress. In turn, however, these stresses are reflected within the balance sheet and should, at least in part, be muted through a recapitalization downward of both land

and building values and therefore ultimately be alleviated somewhat through a lower level of debt service.

There have been many approaches, both local and national, toward subsidy mechanisms for rehabilitating low-income, low-rent housing units. What makes New York City singular, however, is that these same subsidy mechanisms for rehabilitation have been applied to a very broad economic range of housing types and indeed have been most successfully utilized for nominally higher rental units. In essence New York City, in terms of the J51 rehabilitation program, is subsidizing a very broad economic range. Why?

Certainly the realities of rent control as implemented by New York City over the last thirty years play a major role here. Limitations on rents have been significant factors causing reductions in basic maintenance and in retarding private upgrading of facilities. The abortment of normal market forces that would have encouraged landlords to improve their facilities in an effort to secure increased rent rolls and compete for tenantry clearly has led to a crisis of housing quality. Old buildings with new money can be maintained indefinitely; without that vital capital input they will degenerate over time. The J51 program as implemented in New York City must be viewed as one of the costs of rent control, of trying to return the means of housing reinvestment (and to compensate for deferred maintenance) previously denied by rent increase restrictions.

New York City has long passed the conventional model of housing reality in the United States—one in which the large bulk of housing is built by private means within the bounds of municipal tax loads and shaped essentially by market demand on the one hand and federal tax legislation on the other. As data in the Appendix indicate, the pattern of New York City housing starts in the years shown has moved from one in which the private market dominated to one in which subsidies of various kinds became a convention of the field. Rather than the city's housing inputs being forced to meet the cost of the market, the reality has been that an ever increasing variety of subsidy mechanisms has been interposed. Overlooked in the course of this process was one basic phenomenon: A subsidy to everybody is a subsidy to nobody.

Organizational Scheme

The study begins with descriptions of the three major housing programs in New York City that entail the use of restricted property taxation in order to encourage investment in housing (Chapter 2, The Program Context). From these three programs—J51, 421, and Mitchell-Lama—and given the scope of this effort, the 421 program is then selected for detailed analysis. The conceptual outline of this task is initially presented (Chapter 3, The Evaluation Framework) and is then fully operationalized with actual and "best estimate" parameters (Chapter 4, Determining the Fiscal Impact of the 421 Program). Full and detailed calculations of the various fiscal impacts are undertaken, and subsequently aggregated to ascertain total program impacts under alternative situations (Chapter 5, Conclusions: The Total Impact). Conclusions are made about the impact of the program in light of assumed probabilities in the likelihood of each of these situations. Using these results, we then infer the probable impact of the J51 program in comparison to results of the 421 program. An appendix provides a comparison between private and public (and government-assisted private) housing efforts from 1963 to 1974.

Chapter 2

The Program Context

Introduction

Real property taxes are a major component of the cost of operating housing.[3] New York City can therefore use its taxing power to encourage investment in real property by reducing the tax burden on new or existing structures. Several programs have incorporated such tax incentives in order to stimulate housing investment by the private sector. The *J51 program* provides tax exemptions and tax abatements for upgrading of and conversion to multiple dwellings. The *421 program* grants partial tax exemptions for newly constructed multiple dwellings, and has recently been amended to provide benefits to rehabilitated dwellings.[4] Tax exemptions under J51 and 421 are applicable only to that portion of assessed value added to sites or parcels by new construction or rehabilitation. The *Mitchell-Lama program* grants tax exemptions and also provides below market interest rate mortgages to limited-profit and nonprofit investors, with the rate of exemption depending on the type of sponsor. The following portion of this chapter examines each of these programs in more detail.

Tax Exemption for New Multiple Dwellings (421)

Section 421 of the Real Property Tax Law of the State of New York has been in effect since 1971. Its objective has been to stimulate the construction of new multiple dwelling units.[5]

ELIGIBILITY

Prior to 1975, only new multiple dwelling units in structures containing ten or more units were eligible, but the law has been amended to include new or rehabilitated multiple dwellings with six or more units on which construction begins after January 1, 1975, but before January 1, 1978, and which is completed no later than December 31, 1979.[6]

Since 1975, the law has specified that at least 10 percent of the units in projects of 100 or more units contain 4½ rooms. This revision is evidently a response to the program's having been historically skewed toward studio and one-bedroom units.

Eligibility for tax exemption also requires that construction take place on vacant, predominantly vacant, or underutilized land, or on land improved with a nonconforming use. A 1975 amendment specified that in the case of displacement of an existing multiple dwelling with at least twenty units, the newly constructed structure must contain at least five units for every previously occupied unit in existence on December 31, 1974.

PROVISIONS

Partial tax exemption. A declining rate of tax exemption for completed projects is allowed for a period of not more than ten years on that part of assessed valuation added to the property through new construction (or rehabilitation).[7]

The partial exemption rates are as follows:

First two years: full exemption of increased assessed value

Second two years: 80 percent exemption of increased assessed value

Third two years: 60 percent exemption of increased assessed value

Fourth two years: 40 percent exemption of increased assessed value

Fifth two years: 20 percent exemption of increased assessed value

Regulation of rents. Prior to 1975, it was specified that rents be 15 percent below market rates on comparable newly constructed units and that the rents be subject to rent stabilization for a period of ten years or until stabilization is no longer in effect, whichever is shorter. It was the responsibility of the New York City Housing and Development Administration (HDA) to certify that rents were 15 percent below market levels prior to the granting of tax exemptions. Since 1975, initial adjusted monthly rents and comparative monthly rents that would have been paid in the absence of tax exemption have to be determined by the Department of Development prior to the issuance of a certificate of eligibility for partial tax exemption. The adjusted initial monthly rent is to be determined in accordance with a formula spelled out in the law.[8]

Publication of reasonable costs. Since Section 421 was amended in 1975, the Department of Development has been given the responsibility of publishing schedules of reasonable construction costs, as well as of operating and maintenance costs. The Department of Development was still in the process of developing these schedules at the time of this writing and, consequently, no applications had yet been processed under the new law.[9]

PROGRAM PERFORMANCE

The findings reported in this section were secured from a study undertaken for the New York City Housing and Development Administration prior to the recent renewal and revision of the 421 program in August of 1975.[10]

Buildings have been receiving partial tax exemptions under Section 421 since 1971. As of early 1975, the program involved a total of 247 projects with 28,900 units—of which 10,800 were completed and 14,500 were under construction, with applications pending on the remaining 3,600 units.

Since the inception of the 421 program, the bulk of privately financed new construction in New York City has been receiving partial tax exemption benefits: *90 percent of private multiple family dwelling units started from 1971 through 1974 were built under the 421 program.* The program has had most of its impact in Manhattan and Queens. Of the 247 projects in the program, 38 percent are located in Manhattan and 43 percent in Queens. However, given the greater density of Manhattan construction, 63 percent of the units are located there with only 28 percent in Queens. A small amount of lower density construction took place in Staten Island, with the Bronx and Brooklyn having even lower levels of program participation.

The recent revision of 421 has extended eligibility to smaller projects. (Now a six-unit minimum replaces the previous ten-unit minimum.) It is expected that this provision will help to increase program participation in the outer boroughs. As of December 1975, approximately thirty new applications for partial tax exemption had been received, all of them for smaller buildings located predominantly in Queens and Staten Island.[11]

Tax Exemption—Tax Abatement (J51)

Since 1955, section J51-2.5 of the Administrative Code of the City of New York, most recently amended in 1975 by Local Law 859-a, has provided for tax exemption and tax abatement benefits to encourage rehabilitation of existing multiple dwellings and conversion of structures to multiple dwellings. The law was originally designed to eliminate unhealthy or unsafe housing conditions, but over the years its scope has expanded so that it currently encourages general upgrading (in addition to elimination of unhealthy or unsafe conditions), as well as expansion of the number of multiple dwellings through conversion.

ELIGIBILITY

Although the law was previously restricted to existing, structurally sound multiple dwellings, and to conversion of hotels,[12] rooming houses, or one- and two-family structures to multiple dwellings, the recent revision broadens eligibility to buildings consisting of one or two units over commercial space and buildings converted from nonresidential use to multiple dwellings. Prior to 1975, only nonprofit condominiums and cooperatives were eligible among owner occupied properties; however, benefits are now extended to privately financed condominiums and cooperatives rehabilitated within five years after filing the initial prospectus.

As of 1976, the restriction that total assessed valuation prior to improvement not exceed $70 per square foot was removed, thus allowing for rehabilitation of a greater range of properties. Under the current law, however, maximum dollar amounts of abatement are being established for privately financed units.

PROVISIONS

Tax abatement—tax exemption. Any increase in assessed value resulting from the program is exempt from local property taxation for a period of twelve years. Real property taxes are abated by an amount not to exceed 8⅓ percent of the certified reasonable cost of rehabilitation, as determined by the Department of Development, for a period of not less than nine years and not more than twenty years. Total abatement may not exceed 90 percent of the certified reasonable cost of rehabilitation. The 1975 amendment authorized the Department of Development to establish maximum dollar amounts of abatement per dwelling unit for privately financed units.[13]

Regulation of rents. In exchange for tax abatement and tax exemption benefits, buildings are to be placed under either rent control, rent stabilization, or regulation by the United States Department of Housing and Urban Development. It has been administrative policy that where rehabilitation has led to increases in rents, rents are to be rolled back by an amount equal to two-thirds of the first year's tax abatement. This policy has not been entirely effective because of vacancy decontrol and administrative delays.

Bedroom requirements. It is required that converted buildings contain bedrooms of a number equal to at least 50 percent of the apartments created. Excepted from this requirement are buildings converted from nonresidential use where units contain, on average, a floor area of 1,000 square feet.

Filing period. Application for certification of costs must be made within three years following completion of the improvements. However, a "grandfather clause" allowed applications for certification of costs for rehabilitation completed between March 1, 1955 and January 1, 1971 to be filed as late as December 31, 1973.

PROGRAM PERFORMANCE

Findings reported in this section were secured from a study undertaken for HDA prior to the 1976 renewal of the J51 program.[14]

Since 1961, more than 11,000 buildings (totaling approximately 284,000 dwelling units) have participated in the J51 program. Most of the participating buildings have undergone only minor rehabilitation during which tenants could remain in occupancy. (Minor rehabilitation includes installation of fireproof doors and stairs, upgrading or conversion of incinerators, installation of brass plumbing, and rewiring—items clearly consistent with the original objective of improving health and safety conditions.[15]) A relatively small percent of buildings underwent major rehabilitation that necessitated the removal of tenants. However, such buildings (those undergoing "gut" rehabilitation) accounted for the bulk of the certified costs. Between 1967 and 1973, only 15 percent of the participating buildings underwent major rehabilitation, but these same structures accounted for 72 percent of the certified costs for that period.

There has been a general increase in the number of buildings entering the program since its inception, with only a few hundred annually in the earlier years but current levels ranging between 1,500 or 2,000 per year. A broadening of eligibility requirements should continue to increase the number of buildings in the program. Certified costs have been rising not only because of the broadening of eligibility over time, but also because of inflation in the cost of improvements.

Program participation is weighted toward Manhattan, which accounted for 60 percent of certified costs between 1967 and 1973. Major rehabilitation is concentrated in Manhattan even more than is minor rehabilitation—77 percent of all major rehabilitation undertakings in the 1967-73 period were in that borough. Major rehabilitation in Manhattan has been predominantly privately financed, while in other boroughs (primarily the Bronx and Brooklyn) it is predominantly publicly financed, either by New York City or the Federal Housing Administration. The concentration of major rehabilitation in Manhattan reflects, to a large extent, the historically stronger market demand for housing, the bulk of these buildings being located in the prospering areas of the Upper East Side, the Upper West Side, and Chelsea.

Major rehabilitation has been associated with large increases in rents. For privately financed projects, it has been estimated that rents increased an average of 264 percent before rent-rollback and 242 percent after rollback. For publicly financed buildings, the average increase in rent has been estimated at 124 percent. The sharp increase in rents in privately financed units suggests that there is a substantial difference in the income of tenants occupying the units before and after rehabilitation. A sample of fifteen privately financed buildings in Manhattan that underwent "gut" rehabilitation in 1971 and 1972 had initial average monthly rents of $230 per unit after rollback. The average exemption per unit was approximately $6,000. While owners claimed reasonable costs of $9,800 per unit, HDA granted reasonable costs of only $5,500 per unit.

New York City Finance Administration data indicate that the dollar value of certified costs approved under J51 totaled $265 million between 1956 and 1974. For this period, actual tax abatements totaled $63.8 million, with tax relief exemptions totaling about $44.5 million. As exemptions have expired, the city has gained tax revenues estimated by the Finance Administration to be $1.3 million.

The Limited Profit Housing Companies (Mitchell-Lama)[16]

The Limited Profit Housing Companies Law (Laws of New York, 1955) provides tax exemptions and below market interest rate financing to private sponsors of new construction or rehabilitation of cooperative or rental housing. In exchange for this assistance, the projects are subject to public supervision.

Sponsors may be commercial investors, cooperative associations, or nonprofit membership corporations. Commercial projects are restricted to limited profits.

PROVISIONS

Financing. Commercial developers are required to put up an equity investment equal to 10 percent of project costs. Below market interest rate long-term mortgage loans of up to fifty years are provided by either New York City or New York State. Nonprofit corporations sponsoring housing for the elderly may receive 100 percent financing. Cooperative and nonprofit corporations sponsoring housing for hospital or college staffs may receive 95 percent loans.

State financing is from bond issues of state agencies. City financing is from loans granted by HDA and financed through city bond issues. The interest rate on the mortgage loans is the same as on the bonds issued by the agencies to finance the loans.

Tax exemption. Projects sponsored by nonprofit membership corporations receive full real property tax exemption. Limited profit corporations receive tax exemptions for thirty years on an amount up to 50 percent of assessed value or up to 100 percent of the value of improvements created by the project.

Government supervision. State projects are supervised by the State Division of Housing and Community Renewal and the State Housing Finance Agency. City projects are supervised by the Housing and Development Administration. These governmental agencies supervise construction and management costs, tenant selection, and rent schedules. Rents are set to provide the limited profit sponsor with a 6 percent return on equity. Tenant eligibility is based on income and family size.[17]

PERFORMANCE OF THE NEW YORK CITY MITCHELL-LAMA PROGRAM

As of June 1975, a total of 130 Mitchell-Lama projects had been completed, totaling 49,438 dwelling units. Of these projects, sixty-seven are rental while the remaining sixty-three are cooperatives. In terms of borough location 42 percent of the units are in Manhattan, 22 percent in the Bronx, 24 percent in Brooklyn, and the remaining 11 percent in Queens. An additional twenty-seven projects with 12,342 units were still under construction, with the largest number of projects and units situated in Manhattan; one project was under construction in Staten Island.[18]

The Mitchell-Lama program has had a high incidence of debt service and property tax arrearage despite the interest subsidies and tax exemptions, and despite Mitchell-Lama tenants on average having higher incomes and lower rent-income ratios than other city renters.

A 1972 study of Mitchell-Lama housing and a survey of its tenants indicated that out of 102 occupied projects, seventy-two were in debt service arrears totaling $22.7 million.[19] Since that time, the economic position of real property has eroded substantially; as of May 24, 1976, ninety-two out of 140 occupied projects were in arrears totaling $50.9 million.

The survey of Mitchell-Lama tenants indicated that they had higher incomes and lower rent-income ratios than tenants citywide (Mitchell-Lama tenants had a median income of $12,057 compared to $9,245 for all city renters). The median rent-income ratio for Mitchell-Lama tenants was 18.4 percent excluding surcharges, and 22.4 percent including surcharges.[20] However, the survey indicated that surcharges were not being paid. The rent-income ratio for all city renters was 21.7 percent.

The survey further indicated that elderly tenants in Mitchell-Lama projects had lower incomes and higher rent-income ratios than tenants under sixty-five years of age. The median income of elderly tenants was $7,886 compared to $12,984 annually for tenants under sixty-five years of age. The median rent-income ratio, excluding surcharges, for the elderly was 23.5 percent; including surcharges, the ratio was 29 percent.

THE NEW YORK STATE MITCHELL-LAMA PROGRAM

As of March 31, 1975, seventy-five New York State Mitchell-Lama projects containing 52,566 units had been completed in

New York City while seven projects with 8,272 units were under construction.[21] As of December 1975, only six State Mitchell-Lama projects were in real estate tax arrears (including Co-op City), and Co-op City was the only project clearly in debt service arrears.[22]

Exemption and Abatement Levels for 1974-1975
(See Exhibit 2-1)

For the fiscal year 1974-75, 186 Mitchell-Lama projects were receiving tax exemptions on a total assessed value of $573 million, while somewhat less than 200 parcels in the 421 program were receiving tax exemptions on a total assessed valuation of $133 million.[23] For the same fiscal year, parcels in the J51 program were receiving exemptions on a total assessed valuation of $179 million, and tax abatements totaling $14 million. Real estate taxes foregone as a result of these three programs totaled $65 million.[24] Hence, the total taxes foregone due to both exemptions and abatements amounts to $79 million.

EXHIBIT 2—1

VALUE OF EXEMPTIONS FOR FISCAL YEAR 1974-1975 FOR HOUSING RECEIVING REAL PROPERTY TAX EXEMPTIONS UNDER J51, 421, AND MITCHELL-LAMA HOUSING PROGRAMS

PROGRAM	NUMBER OF PARCELS	VALUE OF EXEMPT PROPERTY
J51	5,504	$178,686,100
421	588 [1]	132,579,300
Mitchell-Lama	186 [2]	572,986,600
Total		$884,252,000 [3]

Notes: 1. This figure includes approximately 400 separately listed condominium units included in one project.
2. This figure is less than the 1973-74 figure of 201 parcels, probably due to merging of projects.
3. Taxes foregone equal $7.35 per $100 of assessed value, or a total of $64,992,000 for all three programs.

Source: *Annual Report of the Tax Commission for Fiscal Year 1974-75,* City of New York, p. 31 (forthcoming). Page proof provided by New York City Finance Administration.

Chapter 3

The Evaluation Framework

Introduction

Program evaluation must be done in the context of program objectives. Program evaluation, however, should not be restricted only to the original set of objectives, since the needs of the city change over time, with existing programs serving new objectives of governmental policy.

While the 421, J51, and Mitchell-Lama programs initially focused on the problem of improving the quantity and quality of housing, they must also be evaluated in terms of alternative policy goals such as stimulating employment in the construction industry or, more broadly, stimulating the local economy either by attracting middle-income tenants to the city or by preventing their exodus.

The Mitchell-Lama program's objectives have been to both upgrade the housing stock and redistribute income toward particular tenant groups.[25] The redistribution of income to tenants of the J51 and 421 programs, as well as of the Mitchell-Lama program, be it a policy objective or not, has occurred. Because the tenants of these projects have been middle- and upper-income households, however, the programs have received much criticism for redistributing income in an undesirable direction.[26]

Subsidizing middle- and upper-income households is itself a controversial objective of governmental policy. However, if these subsidies are viewed not as an end in themselves but as a means to stimulate production of housing and the economy as a whole, and if the stimulative effects are strong enough, the initial subsidies will actually be repaid through the generation of additional property, sales, and income taxes. (These potential tax flows are outlined in the subsequent section on program benefits.) Financial assistance given to more affluent households, on this base, turns out to be not a subsidy on the part of government but rather an efficient investment that not only (more than) pays for itself, but also benefits the private sector with better housing, more jobs, and higher incomes.[27]

In order to determine if these programs' subsidies are an effective investment for the city, i.e, whether the initial subsidies in the form of foregone property taxes are eventually repaid, we have undertaken a fiscal impact analysis of the 421 program. The analysis is first developed descriptively by outlining the costs (tax revenues foregone or other costs incurred) and benefits (tax revenues created) of the program from the viewpoint of New York City's tax coffers.[28] The model is then developed quantitatively, employing hypothetical parameters based wherever possible on actual data available. Where no actual data are available, "best judgment" assumptions are made about costs and benefits (see Chapter 4). *The objective of the quantitative analysis is to provide a flexible framework which can be used to evaluate the 421 program for alternative sets of parameters, as well as to quantify the analysis under what we consider to be the most reasonable set of assumptions. .The results of this analysis strongly suggest that the 421 program more than pays for itself when indirect revenue generation effects are taken into account.*

Program Costs

The costs inherent in a program such as 421 are both quantitative, in terms of *actual tax dollars lost and municipal service costs to new residents,* and qualitative, in terms of the negative effects on *the supply of low-income housing.* Critics of tax abatement and tax exemption programs maintain that much of the affected housing would have been built or rehabilitated even in the absence of abatement and/or exemptions.[29] If such projects had been undertaken even in the absence of governmental support, then the city bears a cost of foregone tax revenues to subsidize owners and/or tenants.[30] In addition, even if the programs do initiate new project ventures, the demolition of previously occupied buildings or displacement of existing tenants in rehabilitated dwellings results in economic burdens being imposed for the most part on lower-income households.[31]

While a certain portion of the projects receiving benefits under these programs would have been undertaken in the absence of subsidy, it is surely the case that investment in new and existing housing has been stimulated to some extent by tax exemptions and tax abatement.[32]

Program Benefits

Under the assumption that at least some of the projects required tax relief in order for rehabilitation or new construction to take place, the potential stream of benefits may be substantial. *Assessed values of real property are increased,* so that the nonexempt portion of increased value (421, Mitchell-Lama) or expired exemptions generates revenues to the city in the form of *real property taxes.* Middle-income or upper-income households may be attracted to or induced to remain in the city, generating additional *income and sales taxes* for the city.[33] Spending by these households could lead to an *expansion of commercial space and to increased property tax revenues.* Net migration inward and expansion of commercial space, however, increase the level and cost of municipal services, at least partially offsetting these benefits.[34] The actual spending on construction and rehabilitation will generate not only *employment opportunities* in the local economy, but *also sales and income tax revenues* to the city, subject, of course, to some leakages when spending goes to workers who are not city residents or for goods which are purchased outside the city.[35]

In addition, subsidized new construction or rehabilitation may create *neighborhood externalities* that actually induce the *upgrading of adjacent parcels* without any additional subsidies. Finally, any spending on construction or by tenants that would not have taken place in the absence of subsidies generates *multiplier effects on income and employment* as initial spending is respent by recipients, so that just as employment and income are multiplied upward, tax revenues to the city are multiplied upward from *secondary sales, income, and property tax generation.*

A housing program or set of housing programs alone is not adequate to stimulate the economy as a whole. If, however, such programs are a part of a broad spectrum of governmental policies to revitalize a sagging economy, then these programs can claim partial credit for long run stimulation of new households and firms in addition to the stimulative effects discussed directly above. Again, city tax revenues are indirectly benefited by the initial subsidy to new construction or rehabilitation.

Crucial determinants of the extent to which these programs generate benefits to the city are their impact on rates of return, which induce investment that would not otherwise have taken place, the sensitivity of households to differences in rent when choosing between residing inside or outside the city, and the scale of the programs or overall governmental policy to stimulate both housing and employment.

Indirect program beneficiaries would include those tenants who live in housing *previously* occupied by 421, J51, or Mitchell-Lama tenants; that is, other households may find that housing is filtering down to them as it is vacated by program participants.[36] At a time when it is difficult to either build or rehabilitate housing for lower-income families, given current costs and current levels of subsidy, the provision of housing for more affluent households of the city may be an efficient way of increasing the supply of older and less costly housing to lower-income households.[37] Of course, any benefits from filtration may be offset by displacement of existing tenants because of demolition or major rehabilitation. The costs and benefits to the city discussed above are summarized in Exhibit 3-1.[38]

EXHIBIT 3–1

COSTS AND BENEFITS TO THE CITY ASSOCIATED WITH TAX EXEMPTION OR TAX ABATEMENT PROGRAMS

Costs	Benefits
*Taxes foregone through abatement or exemption **Added costs of municipal services for families who would otherwise not reside in the city Administrative costs	**Taxes generated on non-exempt portion of increased value and on expired exemptions **Income and sales taxes generated by households that would not otherwise locate in city **Property taxes generated by expansion of commercial facilities to meet additional spending **Real estate taxes generated on upgraded adjacent parcels **Sales and income taxes generated by construction spending **Taxes generated by multiplier effects of construction spending and spending by tenants who would not otherwise reside in city Filing fees

Notes: *Applies only to projects that would have been undertaken in absence of exemptions or abatements.
**Applies only to projects that would *not* have been undertaken in absence of exemptions or abatement. Otherwise, benefit or cost is not a result of government subsidy.

The Total Program Impact

The analysis of the fiscal impacts of the 421 program has been undertaken using alternative assumptions about the program's ability both to induce residents to move into or remain in the city and to induce builders to supply units that would not otherwise have been constructed. *The net fiscal impact is established as the present discounted value of costs and benefits for the period 1975 through 1999. Units are assumed to receive partial tax exemption from 1975 through 1984, while indirect program costs and benefits to the city extend through 1999. An 8 percent discount rate is applied to all future costs and revenues to determine the present discounted value as of 1975.*

Included in this analysis are the costs of foregone tax revenues for units that *would have been built* without tax exemption benefits, as well as revenues (taxes) created for the nonexempt portion of increased assessed value on units that *otherwise would not have been built*. (These flows last from 1975 through 1984.) Taxes generated (revenues) from expired exemptions on units that would otherwise not have been built are also taken into account. (These flows last from 1985 through 1999.)

Injections of income and sales taxes from households induced to remain in or move into the city as a result of the program, real estate taxes generated from expansion of commercial space to meet additional spending by these households, and the cost of added municipal services for these households are included. For units that would not have been built, the induced construction spending will itself generate multiplier effects to the extent that it goes into and out of the pockets of other city residents and firms. These multiplier effects, as well as those generated by the spending of households that would not otherwise have located in the city, are also included in the analysis. It should be emphasized, however, that the construction injection occurs only once, while a stream of multiplier effects is generated each year.

Upgrading effects on adjacent parcels are not taken into account, not because the significance of this factor should be minimized, particularly in selected areas, but rather because it requires extended analysis beyond the parameters of this study.[39]

Alternative assumptions are made about the percentage of units induced by the program, the percentage of units occupied by tenants who would not otherwise reside in the city, and whether or not expansion of municipal services and commercial space occurs as a result of occupancy by additional households that would not otherwise have entered the city. While marginal increases in the number of households can be accommodated with given commercial and municipal service levels, after a certain point it is necessary to expand facilities. Because the point at which expansion becomes necessary is unknown, calculations are made with and without these long run effects.[40] The fact that many 421 projects include commercial space suggests that additional households *do* require additional commercial services, although part of this new commercial space may be replacing facilities eliminated by the new construction or reduced elsewhere in the city.

The primary determinant of program impact depends upon whether the unit (or building) would have been built in the absence of tax exemption benefits. For units that would have been built even in the absence of the program, the only net impact on the city is the cost of foregone real estate tax revenues on the exempt portion of the increased assessed value of the parcel. Even though such units may attract or keep new households, or otherwise stimulate the economy, such effects would have occurred without the program and may not represent sufficient gain to offset the cost of the tax exemptions. A reasonable assumption is that one-third to one-half of the units in 421 would not have been built in the absence of tax exemption benefits.[41]

Only those units that would *not* have been built in the absence of the tax exemptions are capable of generating revenues for the city beyond what the free market would have provided. Hence, only in those units do we distinguish whether or not the new construction is occupied by a tenant who would otherwise have left the city or who was induced to move into the city due to the availability of the newly constructed units. In the absence of any data on the previous residence of 421 tenants or what their plans would have been if new housing had not been available, it is assumed that one-third to one-half of the residents of 421 housing either came from outside the city or were previous city residents who would have left the city had no new housing been available.

The operationalization of this basic analytical scheme is the task of the next two chapters. Chapter 4 establishes each of the impacts discussed above, presenting all of the detailed calculations, while Chapter 5 aggregates them in a series of alternative configurations based on various assumptions and probabilities.

Chapter 4

Determining the Fiscal Impacts of the 421 Program

Introduction

This chapter describes the detailed calculations necessary to compute the fiscal impact as presented in Exhibit 3-1. Determination of the following items is included:

1. Real estate taxes foregone or created due to the partial tax exemption
2. Generation of tax revenues through induced construction spending [42]
3. Generation of tax revenues through multiplier effects of induced construction spending
4. Net injection of sales and income taxes by an induced resident [43]
5. Generation of tax revenues through multiplier effects of net spending by induced residents
6. Generation of real property taxes through expansion of commercial space due to spending by induced residents
7. Estimation of the per capita cost of common municipal services

For units that would have been built even in the absence of program benefits, only item 1 (taxes foregone) is relevant.

For units that would not otherwise have been built, item 1 (taxes created) is relevant, as well as items 2 and 3. If the unit is occupied by a resident who would not otherwise have resided in the city, items 4 through 7 enter into the analysis.

The analysis is based on the assumption that a dwelling unit's assessed value increases to $20,000, that construction costs per unit total $30,000, and that the typical household in residence comprises two persons whose gross income before taxes is $25,000 and whose monthly rent is $450.

Real Estate Taxes Foregone or Created Due to Partial Tax Exemption

The 421 program exempts from real property taxation declining portions of the increased assessed value of a parcel as a result of new construction. Exhibit 4-1 details the calculations required to establish taxes which are foregone by the city for a unit that would have been built in the absence of program incentives, and the taxes created for a unit that would not have been built in the absence of the program. In the former case, the city would have received full property taxes on any increase in assessed value; therefore, the partial tax exemption represents a cost to the city.

In the latter case, however, the exemption has stimulated new construction. It must be assumed that no new taxes on increased assessed value would have occurred without the program, because obviously there would not have been an increase in assessed value. The exemption cannot be conceived of as a cost; rather, it must be viewed as a benefit, since the city then receives revenues on the nonexempt portion of increased assessed value. Moreover, once the program provisions terminate (after a ten year period), revenues continue through taxation on the full increase in assessed value.

The present discounted value per unit of taxes foregone if the unit had been built without program incentives is $9,010 (see Exhibit 4-1). The present discounted value of taxes generated by a unit that would not otherwise have been undertaken is equal to $5,463 during the ten year life of the program, but

EXHIBIT 4–1

REAL PROPERTY TAXES PER UNIT FOREGONE[1] OR GENERATED[2] BY THE 421 PARTIAL TAX EXEMPTION PROGRAM, 1975-1999

YEAR	INCREASE IN ASSESSED VALUATION[3]	PARTIAL EXEMPTION RATE[4]	AMOUNT OF EXEMPTION	TAX RATE[5]	YEARLY TAXES FOREGONE	$\frac{1}{(1.08)^t}$ [6]	DISCOUNTED PRESENT VALUE OF TAXES FOREGONE	YEARLY TAXES CREATED	DISCOUNTED PRESENT VALUE OF TAXES CREATED
1975	$20,000	1.00	$20,000	.0819	$ 1,638	1.0000	$1,638	$ 0	$ 0
1976	20,000	1.00	20,000	.0860	1,720	.9259	1,592	0	0
1977	20,000	.80	16,000	.0903	1,445	.8573	1,239	361	309
1978	20,000	.80	16,000	.0948	1,517	.7938	1,204	379	301
1979	20,000	.60	12,000	.0995	1,194	.7350	878	796	585
1980	20,000	.60	12,000	.1045	1,254	.6806	853	836	569
1981	20,000	.40	8,000	.1098	878	.6802	553	1,318	830
1982	20,000	.40	8,000	.1152	922	.5835	538	1,382	806
1983	20,000	.20	4,000	.1210	484	.5403	261	1,936	1,046
1984	20,000	.20	4,000	.1270	508	.5002	254	2,032	1,017
					$11,560		$9,010	$9,040	$ 5,463
1985-1999	20,000/yr	0	0	.1300			—	2,600/yr	11,133[7]

Present Value = $9,010

Present Value = $16,596

(Continued on page 30)

Notes: 1. If the unit would have been built in the absence of tax exemption benefits, then the city foregoes real estate taxes on the exempt portion of the increased assessed value. After 1984, the property receives no exemptions.

2. If the unit would *not* have been built in the absence of tax exemption, then the city gains real estate taxes on the non-exempt portion of the increased assessed value for the ten years of the program and on the full amount of the increased assessed value once the exemptions have completely expired. These benefits are assumed to extend until 1999.

30

EXHIBIT 4–1 (Continued)

REAL PROPERTY TAXES PER UNIT FOREGONE[1] OR GENERATED[2] BY THE 421 PARTIAL TAX EXEMPTION PROGRAM, 1975-1999

3. The per dwelling increase in assessed value due to new construction is assumed to be $20,000. A recent study of the 421 program found the increase for buildings in the program from 1971 to 1974 to be approximately $14,000. (Jacob Ukeles et al., *An Assessment of the ∫421 Limited Tax Exemption Program*, Interim Report, Department of Urban Affairs and Policy Analysis, Center for New York City Affairs, New School for Social Research, p. 32. Increased assessed value must be calculated from data on this page.) The assessed value of $20,000 that we present is more reflective of the 1975 Manhattan housing market in which the typical tenant is assumed to reside.

4. The partial tax exemption rates are as specified in the 421 law.

5. The real estate tax rate is assumed to grow at a rate of 5 percent per year through 1984. (This is somewhat below its historical rate of increase in the previous ten year period). To calculate taxes created after the expiration of exemptions in 1984, we assume a constant real estate tax rate of $13 per $100 of assessed value.

6. A discount rate of 8 percent is employed. This assumes some moderation of the city's current money costs, though historically it is on the high side. The present value is obtained by use of a present worth factor $\frac{1}{(1.08)^t}$ where t=0 in 1975, 1 in 1976, etc.

7. Present discounted value using the 8 percent discount rate of an annual stream of $2,600 for a 15-year period (1985-1999).

Present value 1985 (beginning of term 1985 = end of term 1984):

$$\$2600 \frac{(1+.08)^{15}-1}{.08(1+.08)^{15}}$$

$$\$2600 \ (8.560) = \$22,256$$

Present Value 1975, where 1975 = year 0:

$$\$22,256 \ \frac{1}{(1+.08)^9}$$

$$\$22,256 \ (.5002) = \$11,133$$

this total increases to $16,596 if the taxes generated in the ensuing fifteen year period—after the exemptions expire—are also taken into account. (It is thus assumed that the economic life of a project is twenty-five years.)

The calculations employ the actual partial exemption schedule in the current 421 law (100 percent in the first two years, and 80 percent, 60 percent, 40 percent, and 20 percent in each of the four subsequent two year periods). The real estate tax rate is assumed to increase at 5 percent per annum through 1984 (somewhat below its rate of increase over the past ten years), but is assumed to remain at $13 per $100 of assessed value for the period 1985 through 1999. An 8 percent discount rate is employed; this may be thought of as the cost of money to the city. We further assume that the city's ability to borrow will return to normal in the near future.[44]

An assessed value increase of $20,000 per unit is assumed. A recent study of the 421 program indicated a $14,000 increase in assessed value for units entering the program from 1971 through 1974.[45] We have inflated this figure to represent more adequately the 1975 market.

Generation of Tax Revenues Through Induced Construction Spending[46]

It is estimated that the construction costs of a typical unit are approximately $30,000.[47] Construction spending on labor and materials not only stimulates the local economy, but also contributes direct tax revenues through taxation of the initial round of spending and through taxation of additional spending due to multiplier effects.[48] We conservatively estimate that one-half of the expenditures for labor accrues to city residents and the other half to nonresidents. We also assume that only one-third of the materials expenditures is made within the city since there is a strong incentive to avoid the New York City sales tax. *If 40 percent of the construction bill goes toward labor and 45 percent goes toward materials,*[49] *then the total tax contribution of the initial round of spending on construction is equal to $303* (see Exhibit 4-2).

EXHIBIT 4–2

ESTIMATED TAX REVENUES GENERATED DIRECTLY FROM INDUCED CONSTRUCTION SPENDING

Estimated Construction Cost $=$ \$30,000[b]

Labor Costs $=$ .40 X \$30,000 $=$ \$12,000[c]

    Labor Income to City Residents $=$ .5 X \$12,000 $=$ \$6,000[a]

    Income Taxes Paid on Labor Income by City Residents $=$
    .016[d] X \$6,000 $=$ \$ 96

    Labor Income to Non-City Residents $=$ .5 X \$12,000 $=$ \$6,000[a]

    Income Taxes Paid on Labor Income by Non-Residents $=$
    .0045[e] X \$6,000 $=$ \$ 27

Cost of Materials $=$ .45 X \$30,000 $=$ \$13,500[c]

    Materials Purchased in City $=$ .33 X \$13,500 $=$ \$4,500[a]

    City Sales Taxes on Purchased Materials $=$ .08 X \$4,500 $=$ \$180

Total Taxes Accruing to the City from
Construction Spending $=$ \$303

Notes: a. The projection assumes that one-half of the labor income goes to city residents and that one-third of the materials is purchased locally.

      b. Based on data for Mitchell-Lama housing under construction on March 31, 1975. A 4.4 room unit has an estimated construction cost of \$41,000 or \$9,400 per room. (Division of Housing and Community Renewal, *Statistical Summary of Programs,* New York State, March 31, 1975, p. 65.) We increase the per room figure to account for smaller units in 421 housing and for their luxury nature. Our estimate of \$30,000 per unit is probably on the low side.

      c. A McKinsey study of new construction indicates that construction costs for conventionally financed units may be divided into labor costs of 40 percent, material costs of 45 percent, and overhead and profit totaling 15 percent. (McKinsey & Company, *Defining Potential City Initiatives in the Stimulation of Private New Residential Construction,* New York, October 1, 1969.)

      d. Estimated average tax rate on before-tax income.

      e. Actual nonresident income tax rate.

Generation of Tax Revenues Through Multiplier Effects of Induced Construction Spending[50]

If a dwelling unit has a construction cost of \$30,000 and if we assume a local multiplier of 1.67 (which is comparable to a conservative 0.4 marginal propensity to consume locally),[51] then the induced income generation of this initial injection is equal to another $20,000. It is estimated that approximately 8 percent of local spending returns to the city as tax revenue through sales, income, and property taxation.[52] (It is this taxation itself that helps to limit the multiplier effect; that is, taxes are a leakage from the spending stream.) Hence, induced spending effects eventually generate $1,600 in tax revenues. The multiplier from construction spending does not work itself out immediately, so we spread this $1,600 over a three year period and then discount it back to present value using an 8 percent discount rate. *The result is a contribution of $1,484 to the fiscal impact of any unit that would not otherwise have been built* (see Exhibit 4-3).

EXHIBIT 4–3

DETERMINATION OF PRESENT VALUE OF TAX REVENUES DERIVED FROM MULTIPLIER EFFECTS OF CONSTRUCTION COST

$$\text{Present Value} = \sum_{t=0}^{2} 533.33 \left(\frac{1}{1.08}\right)^t$$

t	Tax Revenues	$\left(\frac{1}{1.08}\right)^t$	Present Value
0	$533.33	1.0000	$533.33
1	533.33	.9259	493.82
2	533.33	.8573	457.22

$$\Sigma = \$1,484$$

$$\text{Present Value} = \underline{\$1,484}$$

Net Injection of Sales and Income Taxes by an Induced Resident[53]

We assume that the typical 421 family is composed of two adults earning a total annual income, before taxes, of $25,000. Its typical budget, presented in Exhibit 4-4, is determined by calculating actual city, state, and federal taxes for the family (using a standard deduction and two exemptions). A rent of $450 per month is assumed, which closely approximates the cost of a one-bedroom unit in a 421 building; monthly utility payments are estimated at $25. Expenditures on food at home and food away from home are based on data in the "1972 Diary Data" from the *Consumer Expenditure Survey Series* of the United States Bureau of Labor Statistics. Adjustments to this allocation for a two-person household with an income of $25,000 or more are made in order to account for the family's living in a Northeastern SMSA. This total is then increased to account for increasing food prices, but with a somewhat reduced volume of consumption to reflect a 1975 budget (see Exhibit 4-5). The telephone outlay is a rough estimate. All other items are approximated by using data from the autumn 1974 four-person *City Worker Family Budget for New York-Northeastern New Jersey* prepared by the Bureau of Labor Statistics, with some adjustments made to account for a two-person household.

We assume that even if the household did not initially reside in the city, it would still have been employed there. (The 421 program affects housing choices, but not job choices.) Therefore, the net injection of income taxes is equivalent to the difference between resident income taxes and nonresident taxes. Resident income taxes are calculated to be $451, while the nonresident taxes on an equivalent household would be only $112. *Hence, net injection of income taxes by an induced resident is equal to $339* (see Exhibit 4-6).

Net sales tax injection is calculated to take into account those items subject to sales taxes in the budget appearing in Exhibit 4-4. Corrections are made, however, to account for expenditures made outside the city as well as for expenditures made in the city that would have been made there even if the household had resided elsewhere. A 15 percent reduction is made in the categories of food away from home and miscellaneous taxable items to account for expenditures outside the city (most likely to occur during vacations).[54] An adjustment is made to telephone expenses to reflect only the local portion of

EXHIBIT 4–4
ESTIMATED ANNUAL HOUSEHOLD BUDGET, TWO-PERSON HOUSEHOLD, TOTAL INCOME OF $25,000

Expenditure Category	Dollars	Percent of Total
Income Taxes [1]		
Federal	$4,668	18.7
State	1,651	6.6
City	451	1.8
Rent	5,400	21.6
*Utilities	300	1.2
*Telephone [2]	240	1.0
Food at Home [3]	1,800	7.2
*Food Away from Home [3]	1,800	7.2
*Clothing and Personal Care	1,600	6.4
Medical Care	700	2.8
Transportation [4]	1,500	6.0
*Miscellaneous Taxable	1,800	7.2
Miscellaneous Non-Taxable [5]	1,100	4.4
Savings	1,990	7.9
TOTAL	$25,000	100.0

Notes:
1. Taxes are calculated assuming two exemptions and a standard deduction for a couple filing jointly.
2. Only $180 of the phone bill is subject to city taxes.
3. Food at home and food away from home are based on data from the *Consumer Expenditure Survey Series, Diary Data 1972,* "Selected Weekly Expenditures Cross-Classified by Family Characteristics." The food categories for a two-person household with $25,000 before-tax income for all U.S. families is adjusted to reflect families in SMSAs in the Northeastern United States using data from that same series and is then increased using the consumer price index for changes in the cost of living between 1972 and 1975 for New York City. The calculations are approximate. (See Exhibit 4-5.)
4. It is assumed that the household owns an automobile which is not garaged, and that it makes outlays for gasoline, maintenance and auto insurance, as well as outlays for public transportation.
5. This includes social security, insurance, and charitable contributions.
6. Estimation of the expenditures on clothing and personal services, medical care, transportation, and miscellaneous taxable and non-taxable items is based on data from the higher level *City Worker Family Budget for New York-Northeastern New Jersey—Autumn 1974,* U.S. Department of Labor, Bureau of Labor Statistics, Middle Atlantic Region, Press Release May 27, 1975.
* Subject to 4 percent city sales tax. See calculation of city sales tax contribution in Exhibit 4-6.

EXHIBIT 4–5

ESTIMATED EXPENDITURES ON FOOD AT HOME AND FOOD AWAY FROM HOME

Weekly Expenditures on Food, Family of Two, Before-Tax Income of $25,000+

	U.S. RURAL AND URBAN [1]	ADJUSTED TO NORTHEAST (INSIDE SMSAs) [2]	ADJUSTED TO 1975 [3]
Food at Home	$24.39	$27.90	$35
Food Away from Home	$23.28	$27.96	$35

Notes: 1. *Consumer Expenditure Survey Series: Diary Data 1972,* Bureau of Labor Statistics, U.S. Department of Labor, Report 448-1, Table 2. Data collected for the period July 1972-June 1973.

2. Using data from Table 15 in source cited above, it was found that for all family sizes and incomes, expenditures for food at home for families living inside SMSAs in the northeast were 14.4 percent higher than for all U.S. families. Hence we increase the U.S. urban and rural figure for two-person families with incomes of $25,000 or more by 14.4 percent to reflect the northeast SMSA situation. A similar upward adjustment of 20.1 percent is made to the food away from home figure of the U.S. rural and urban family of two with an income of $25,000 or more to adjust it to the northeast SMSA context.

3. Between June 1973 and June 1975, the Consumer Price Index for urban wage earners and clerical workers in the New York-Northeastern New Jersey region increased by 18.8 percent. Since food prices were rising more rapidly than all items, we have increased the budgets by 25 percent to reflect rising prices with a small reduction in quantity consumed. (As prices of certain items rise relative to others, even though total expenditure on the item may be rising, there may actually be a reduced level of consumption.) Between June 1973 and December 1974, the food index for the country as a whole rose by more than 21 percent. Projecting this monthly rate of increase to the end of June 1975 would yield a rate of inflation in food prices from June 1973 to June 1975 of more than 28 percent.

EXHIBIT 4–6

ESTIMATED FEDERAL, STATE, AND LOCAL INCOME TAXES FOR HOUSEHOLD OF TWO, INCOME OF $25,000, ASSUMING THE STANDARD DEDUCTION AND TWO EXEMPTIONS

FAMILY OF TWO

Income = $25,000

$ 450 Monthly contract rent
  25 Monthly utilities
$ 475 Monthly gross rent
5,700 Annual gross rent
.228 Gross Rent/Income Ratio

INCOME TAXES CALENDAR YEAR 1975 (FILING JOINT RETURN)

Federal Taxes

$25,000	Income (Gross)
2,600	Standard Deduction
1,500	Exemption: 2 X $750
$20,900	Adjusted Gross Income

Schedule Y, Filing Jointly
Adjusted Gross Category: $20,000—24,000
Tax = $4,380 + .32($20,900–20,000)
   = $4,380+$288
Tax = $4,668

State Taxes

$25,000	Income (Gross)
2,000	Standard Deduction
1,300	Exemption: 2 X $650
$21,700	Adjusted Gross Category: $21,000—23,000

Tax = $1,520 + .13($21,700–21,000)
   = $1,520 + $91
Tax = $1,611
Surcharge = $1611 X .025 = $40.27
Tax + Surcharge = $1,651

City Resident Taxes

Nonresident City Taxes
.0045 X $25,000 = $112.50
Tax = $112.50

$25,000	Income (Gross)
1,000	Standard Deduction
1,200	Exemption: 2 X $600
$22,800	Adjusted Gross Catgory: $20,000—25,000

Tax = $373 + .028($22,800–20,000)
   = $373 + $78.40
Tax = $451.40

the bill subject to local taxation. Taxable items are thus totaled after these adjustments have been made, with the total taxable outlay amounting to $5,710. Since the state and city sales tax rates equal 8 percent, the total outlay can be disaggregated to $5,287 for purchases plus $423 in state and local sales taxes. The local share of the sales taxes is $211 (a 4 percent city sales tax rate).[55]

A portion of expenditures would have been made inside the city even if the household resided elsewhere (but was employed within the city). We make the assumption that 15 percent of these sales taxes would have been paid out even if the household were nonresident. Hence, the net injection of city sales taxes is reduced to $179 (see Exhibit 4-7).

Net injection of sales and income taxes by an induced resident total $518 ($339 + $179). *If income and expenditures grow at roughly 6 percent per year, the present discounted value of the flow over twenty-five years (ignoring the progressive nature of changes in city income taxes and changes in city sales taxes) is equal to $10,442, using an 8 percent discount rate*[56] (see Exhibit 4-8).

Generation of Tax Revenues Through Multiplier Effects of Net Spending by Induced Residents[57]

In addition to taxes generated by the household's spending in New York City, the multiplier effects of this spending within the local economy will also (eventually) result in increased revenues for the city. Using a multiplier of 1.67, based on a local marginal propensity to consume of 0.4, the household's initial injection of approximately $14,301 of local spending excluding taxes [58] would result in an additional $9,533 stream of spending. The result of such spending would be approximately another $763 in tax revenues for New York City through real estate, sales, and income taxes.[59] Such a stream would take time to develop (say, two years), so the present discounted value of such a stream would be somewhat less—$707. Such a stream would be generated in each year. Indeed, as money incomes grow, the multiplied tax stream will also grow. *As-*

EXHIBIT 4–7

ESTIMATED NET INJECTION OF SALES TAXES FOR FAMILY OF TWO, ANNUAL INCOME OF $25,000

TAXABLE ITEMS [1]	
Utilities	$ 300
Telephone [2]	180
Food Away from Home [3]	1,530
Clothing and Personal Care [4]	1,600
Miscellaneous Taxable [3]	1,530
Auto Maintenance (including gas) [5]	570
TOTAL	$5,710
Expenditures Excluding 4 Percent City Sales Tax and 4 Percent State Sales Tax $\dfrac{\$5710}{1.08} =$	$5,287
Portion of Expenditures Going to City Sales Tax $= \$5287 \times .04 =$	$ 211
Total City Sales Tax Paid	$ 211
Less 15 percent for expenditures which would have been made as a nonresident	−32
Net Injection of City Sales Taxes	$ 179

Notes:
1. See Exhibit 4-4 for total family budget.
2. Reduced to include only local portion of telephone bill.
3. Reduced by 15 percent to account for expenditures outside the city.
4. Certain personal services such as haircuts were previously not subject to city sales tax. As of 1976 these items carry a 4 percent city levy. Our calculations are approximate so we treat this entire category as if it were subject to 4 percent city tax and 4 percent state tax.
5. It is assumed that the household has $300 in auto maintenance expenses (excluding gasoline), which includes 8 percent city and state sales taxes. The remaining $270 is the cost of gasoline net of all taxes except state and city sales taxes. (It assumes a price of 50 cents per gallon net of all taxes and is based on consumption of 500 gallons of gasoline per year, which is assumed to be the local portion of gasoline purchases. This is equivalent to driving 7500 miles at 15 miles per gallon.) These auto expenses are a subset of the transportation budget in Exhibit 4-4, which includes car insurance as well as outlays for public transportation and taxicabs. While taxi fleets pay sales taxes on fares, the taxi outlay on the household is estimated to be in the range of $50-$75, so taxes generated would be no more than $3 (at the city tax rate of 4 percent). Hence, this amount is small enough to ignore.

40

EXHIBIT 4–8

DETERMINATION OF PRESENT VALUE OF SALES AND INCOME TAXES

$$\text{Present Value} = \sum_{t=0}^{24} 518 \left(\frac{1.06}{1.08}\right)^t$$

t	Sales and Income Taxes	$\left(\frac{1.06}{1.08}\right)^t$	Present Value
0	$518	1.0000	$518.00
1	518	.9815	508.42
2	518	.9633	499.01
3	518	.9455	489.78
4	518	.9280	480.72
5	518	.9109	471.83
6	518	.8940	463.10
7	518	.8775	454.53
8	518	.8612	446.12
9	518	.8453	437.87
10	518	.8297	429.77
11	518	.8143	421.82
12	518	.7993	414.01
13	518	.7845	406.35
14	518	.7699	398.84
15	518	.7557	391.46
16	518	.7417	384.22
17	518	.7279	377.11
18	518	.7145	370.13
19	518	.7013	363.28
20	518	.6883	356.56
21	518	.6756	349.97
22	518	.6631	343.49
23	518	.6508	337.14
24	518	.6388	330.90

$$\Sigma = \$10,442^1$$

Present Value = $10,442

Note: 1. Total Present Value determined from unrounded data.

suming a 6 percent rate of growth of expenditures and an 8 percent discount rate, the present value of the multiplier effects for the period 1975-1999 actually totals $14,252 [60] (see Exhibit 4-9).

EXHIBIT 4–9

DETERMINATION OF PRESENT VALUE OF MULTIPLIER EFFECTS OF SPENDING

$$\text{Present Value} = \sum_{t=0}^{24} 707 \left(\frac{1.06}{1.08}\right)^t$$

t	Multiplier Effects of Spending	$\left(\frac{1.06}{1.08}\right)^t$	Present Value
0	$707	1.0000	$707.00
1	707	.9815	693.92
2	707	.9633	681.08
3	707	.9455	668.48
4	707	.9280	656.12
5	707	.9109	643.98
6	707	.8940	632.06
7	707	.8775	620.37
8	707	.8612	608.89
9	707	.8453	597.63
10	707	.8297	586.57
11	707	.8143	575.72
12	707	.7993	565.07
13	707	.7845	554.62
14	707	.7699	544.36
15	707	.7557	534.29
16	707	.7417	524.40
17	707	.7279	514.70
18	707	.7145	505.18
19	707	.7013	495.83
20	707	.6883	486.66
21	707	.6756	477.66
22	707	.6631	468.82
23	707	.6508	460.15
24	707	.6388	451.63

$$\Sigma = \$14,255^1$$

Present Value = $14,255

Note: 1. Total Present Value determined from unrounded data.

Generation of Real Property Taxes Through Expansion of Commercial Space Due to Spending by Induced Residents

In addition to the sales taxes generated by the spending of induced residents, expanded sales will in the long run result in expansion of commercial space, which will provide additional revenues to the city through the payment of property taxes.[61] We calculated these long run effects on the basis of data concerning the relationship between sales volumes and rents for various spending categories, and then translated the rents to property taxes by assuming that 25 percent of the rent dollar goes toward property taxes. The rent-sales ratio varies with expenditure category. The household budget (Exhibit 4-4), with modifications that restrict it to local outlays (Exhibit 4-7), provides data for increases in sales volume by expenditure category. Exhibit 4-10 shows the increase in spending for each category,[62] the rent-sales ratio, and the increase in property taxes that would result from such spending. Increased property tax payments for telephone and utilities are estimated more directly by applying the ratio of property taxes to total revenues for each of the categories, using the assumption that the firms are in a range of constant long run average costs, in which case marginal costs would be equal to average costs. This is probably a better assumption about telephone and utilities companies, which are in existence because of scale economies and may well be in the range of exhausting such economies.

Total property taxes generated by expansion of commercial space in response to spending by induced residents is equal to $153. While this is a long run effect, if expansion occurs in anticipation of growth (for example, commercial space is usually included along with 421 projects to meet expanded demand), then these long run effects may be assumed to begin at the same time that the 421 program commences. Hence, when the fiscal impact analysis is carried out, the expansion of commercial space is assumed to enter the analysis simultaneously with the flow of increased spending by induced residents.[63]

EXHIBIT 4–10

ESTIMATED GENERATION OF REAL PROPERTY TAXES THROUGH EXPANSION OF COMMERCIAL SPACE DUE TO SPENDING BY INDUCED RESIDENTS[a]

Items	Annual Expenditure of Typical Household[b]	Estimated Ratio of Rent to Sales	Ratio of Property Taxes to Rent	Estimated Increase in Real Property Taxes of Seller
Utilities	$ 300			$ 30[d]
Telephone	240			19[e]
Food at Home	1,800	.03	.25	13
Food Away from Home	1,530[c]	.08	.25	31
Clothing and Personal Care	1,600	.08	.25	32
Medical Care	700	.05	.25	9
Miscellaneous Taxable	1,530[c]	.05	.25	19
				$153

Notes:
a. The basic assumption is that expanded demand for goods and services leads to expansion of commercial facilities and to increases in real property taxes. While these are long run effects, expansions of capacity may be made in anticipation of needs; we can assume that expansion of commercial space coincides with expansion of housing through the 421 program. Such effects are considered as benefits of the 421 program only for units that would not otherwise have been built. Expansion of commercial space and of households also requires the city to bear cost of expanded common municipal services. These are also included in the analysis of fiscal impact and are estimated to be $412 per capita.

b. Outlays are based on a two-person household with an annual income of $25,000. See Exhibit 4-4.

c. Reduced by 15 percent from entry in Exhibit 4-4 to account for expenditures outside the city.

d. Approximately 10 percent of revenues of Consolidated Edison are paid out in real property taxes (Charles Kaiser, "Assessing Real Estate for Taxation at 100 Percent of Full Market Value," *New York Times,* 10 March 1976, p. 36.

e. Approximately 8 percent of revenues of New York Telephone are paid out in real property taxes (*New York Telephone Company Annual Report 1974,* p. 6).

If this flow of property tax revenues grows at 5 percent for the period 1975-1984 because of increases in the property tax rate, with stabilization of the rate after that period at around $13 per $100 of assessed value,[64] *the present discounted value of this stream of property taxes discounted back at 8 percent per year is equal to $2,368*[65] (see Exhibit 4-11).

Estimating the Per Capita Cost of Common Municipal Services

It is difficult to determine at just what point additional households begin to cause the expansion of common municipal services. This is probably a step function in which the cost and level of services remain constant over a certain range and then take a discrete jump to a higher level. However, such functions can be approximated by smooth curves. Moreover, if the long run average cost curve of municipal services tends to be in a range of minimum long run average costs (in which all scale economies are being captured) then we can approximate the long run marginal cost of services with the per capita long run cost.

Data on 1973-74 budgetary outlays for New York City are used to determine the per capita cost of common municipal services for that year. Exhibit 4-12 displays this budget and indicates those expenditures that have been included as common municipal functions. These functions, which are basically all those listed except hospitals, education, and debt service, total $2.859 billion. The city population was estimated as 7.794 million as of 1974 (and has fallen since then to approximately 7.6 million). The 1974 average per capita outlay on common municipal services is thus $367. We increase the 1974 estimate by 6 percent to produce the 1975 estimate, a rate reflecting some growth of costs combined with some cutbacks in the level of city services during the current fiscal crisis. Therefore, 1975 per capita costs are estimated to be $389.

If these costs are expected to grow at 6 percent per year, and if they are discounted back at 8 percent per year, then the present discounted value of this item for the period 1975-1999

EXHIBIT 4–11

DETERMINATION OF PRESENT VALUE OF REAL PROPERTY TAXES OF EXPANDED COMMERCIAL SPACE

$$\text{Present Value} = \sum_{t=0}^{9} 153 \left(\frac{1.05}{1.08}\right)^t + \sum_{t=10}^{24} 153 \frac{(1.05)^9}{(1.08)^t}$$

t	Real Property Tax	$\left(\dfrac{1.05}{1.08}\right)^t$	Present Value	$\dfrac{(1.05)^9}{(1.08)^t}$	Present Value
0	$ 153	1.0000	$ 153.00	—	—
1	153	.9722	148.75	—	—
2	153	.9422	144.62	—	—
3	153	.9189	140.59	—	—
4	153	.8934	136.69	—	—
5	153	.8685	132.88	—	—
6	153	.8444	129.19	—	—
7	153	.8209	125.60	—	—
8	153	.7982	122.12	—	—
9	153	.7760	118.73	—	—
10	153	—	—	.7184	109.92
11	153	—	—	.6651	101.76
12	153	—	—	.6160	94.24
13	153	—	—	.5702	87.24
14	153	—	—	.5281	80.80
15	153	—	—	.4890	74.82
16	153	—	—	.4527	69.26
17	153	—	—	.4192	64.14
18	153	—	—	.3881	59.38
19	153	—	—	.3594	54.99
20	153	—	—	.3328	50.92
21	153	—	—	.3081	47.14
22	153	—	—	.2853	43.65
23	153	—	—	.2642	40.42
24	153	—	—	.2446	37.42
			$\Sigma = \$1,352$		$\Sigma = \$1,016$

Present Value = $1,352 + $1,016 = $2,368

EXHIBIT 4–12

NEW YORK CITY EXPENDITURES BY DEPARTMENT GROUPING, FISCAL YEAR 1973-1974

DEPARTMENT	
* Legislative	$ 3,204,134
* General Government, City	225,630,445
* Libraries	42,567,651
Education	2,768,992,125
* Cultural, etc.	13,209,367
* Municipal Parks	64,664,657
* Public Safety	1,125,514,858
* Sanitation, Health	441,484,224
Hospitals	870,045,009
Social Welfare	2,671,080,089
* Correction	89,500,432
* City Judicial	51,397,436
* Public Service	118,796,946
* General Government, County	21,610,300
* Judicial, County	59,416,338
Debt Service	867,551,817
* Miscellaneous	602,062,543
Human Resources Administration	58,475,052
Model Cities Administration	65,000,000
TOTAL	$10,160,203,423
* Subtotal	2,859,059,331

1974 Per Capita Cost = $337 ($2,859,059,331 ÷ 7,794,000)

Note: * Included as cost of common municipal services.
Source: New York Chamber of Commerce and Industry, *New York City Finances: A Ten Year Review 1963-64 1973-74*, Table IX.

is equal to $7,842 per person, or $15,684 per household of two persons (see Exhibit 4-13).

The preceding analyses have established quantitative estimates of each of the seven basic fiscal impacts. It is now possible to determine the total impact under a series of alternative assumptions. This will be the objective of Chapter 5.

EXHIBIT 4–13

DETERMINATION OF PRESENT VALUE
OF COMMON MUNICIPAL SERVICE COSTS

$$\text{Present Value} = \sum_{t=0}^{24} 389 \left(\frac{1.06}{1.08}\right)^t$$

t	Municipal Service Cost	$\left(\frac{1.06}{1.08}\right)^t$	Present Value
0	$ 389	1.0000	$ 389.00
1	389	.9815	381.80
2	389	.9633	374.74
3	389	.9455	367.81
4	389	.9280	361.00
5	389	.9109	354.32
6	389	.8940	347.77
7	389	.8775	341.34
8	389	.8612	335.02
9	389	.8453	328.82
10	389	.8297	322.74
11	389	.8143	316.77
12	389	.7993	310.91
13	389	.7845	305.16
14	389	.7699	299.51
15	389	.7557	293.97
16	389	.7417	288.53
17	389	.7279	283.19
18	389	.7145	277.96
19	389	.7013	272.81
20	389	.6883	267.77
21	389	.6756	262.81
22	389	.6631	257.95
23	389	.6508	253.18
24	389	.6388	248.49

$$\Sigma = \$7,842^1$$

Present Value = $7,842 (per capita)

Note: 1. Total Present Value determined from unrounded data.

Chapter 5

Conclusions:
The Total Impact

Introduction

The results of the preceding analyses can now be aggregated in various combinations to establish the overall impact of the 421 program. The alternative determinations of net fiscal impact are based on five different possible situations:

Case 1: The unit would have been built in the absence of tax exemption benefits.

Case 2: The unit would not have been built in the absence of tax exemption benefits, and the occupying tenant still would have resided *within* the city.

Case 3a: The unit would not have been built in the absence of tax exemption benefits, and the occupying tenant would then have resided *outside* the city although employed within the city. No additional commercial space would be generated and no additional cost of municipal services would be required.

Case 3b: The same as Case 3a, *except* that commercial space would be generated and municipal services costs would be incurred as a result of household expansion and commercial expansion.

Case 3c: The same as Case 3b, *except* that multiplier effects from construction spending and from spending of induced residents is added to the analysis.

Case 1 takes into account only the cost of property taxes foregone through the tax exemption. All other costs or benefits associated with the new construction would have taken place regardless of the program, under the assumption that the units would not have been built in any event.

Case 2 assumes that a unit would not have been built without the tax exemption provisions. Thus, while a portion of the increase in assessed value arising from new construction is exempt from property taxation, the nonexempt portion generates tax revenues during the first ten years of the program; in the ensuing period, taxes are generated on the entire increase in assessed value (once the exemptions have expired). Another benefit accruing from the construction of such a unit is the direct tax impact of construction spending.

Case 3a includes all the benefits included in Case 2, as well as the net injection of sales and income taxes by households that would not otherwise have located in the city, and who are living in units that would not have been built except for the tax exemption benefits. These injections are net of taxes that would be paid by the households if they located outside the city but still worked in the city.

In *Case 3b*, the long term effects of inward migration are taken into account—both the property tax revenues accruing from expansion of commercial space and the costs of added common municipal services that the city must provide in order to meet the needs of increased population and commerce.[66]

Case 3c adds to the items of Case 3b the indirect program benefits resulting from the multiplier effects of initial construction spending and of spending by households that would not otherwise have located in the city. This final case, however, does not take into account the possible increase in costs to the city if these multiplier effects result in increased population with an added cost of municipal services.

The Total Impact

The previous chapter provided a detailed description of how the costs and benefits associated with each of these cases were determined. It is the sum of these costs and benefits for each case that determines the net fiscal impact for each case. The fiscal impacts per unit (present discounted value) for all five cases are displayed in Exhibit 5-1.

Under the most pessimistic assumption—that the unit granted partial tax exemption under section 421 would have been built regardless of the program—the net fiscal impact per unit is equal to $9,010 (Case 1). If the unit would not have been built without tax exemption benefits and if it is occupied by a tenant who would not otherwise have resided within the city, the net fiscal impact per unit is $16,899 (Case 2). Under the more optimistic assumption—that the unit would not have been built and is occupied by a tenant who would not otherwise have resided within the city—the net fiscal impact per unit is equal to $27,341 if no additional commercial space is generated and no additional cost of municipal services is incurred (Case 3a). However, if there is expansion of commercial space and if there is also expansion of municipal services by the households and added commercial space, then the net fiscal impact per unit falls to a level of $14,025 (Case 3b). If the multiplier effects of construction spending and of spending by induced residents are added to the analysis, the fiscal impact of a unit again rises to a high of $29,761 (Case 3c).

By applying alternative sets of probability weights to the impacts for the various cases (3a, 3b, and 3c being treated as mutually exclusive cases), a set of alternative outcomes is calculated (see Exhibit 5-2). Different combinations of probabilities (columns a through l) have been assumed in order to assess the impact of varying shares of 421 program units falling into each case possibility (cases 1, 2, 3a, 3b, and 3c). This exhibit includes not only the most reasonable mix of cases, but also those mixes which yield a break-even outcome; that is, a net fiscal impact in the vicinity of zero.

Since the likelihood of all units falling into either Case 1, Case 2, or Case 3 is extremely low, some reasonable assumptions

EXHIBIT 5-1

PER UNIT FISCAL IMPACT OF THE 421 PROGRAM
UNDER ALTERNATIVE ASSUMPTIONS
(Present Discounted Value, 1975-1999)

			CASES		
FISCAL EFFECTS	1	2	3a	3b	3c
Real Estate Taxes Foregone	−$9,010				
Real Estate Taxes Created		$16,596	$16,596	$16,596	$16,596
Net Sales and Income Tax Injection from Induced Construction		303	303	303	303
Net Sales and Income Tax Injection from Induced Residents			10,442	10,442	10,442
Real Estate Taxes on Expanded Commercial Space				2,368	2,368
Added per Household Cost of Common Municipal Services				−15,684	−15,684
Multiplier Effects of Induced Construction					1,484
Multiplier Effects of Induced Resident's Spending					14,252
Per Unit Net Fiscal Impact (present discounted value)	−$9,010	$16,899	$27,341	$14,025	$29,761

Notes: Cases are defined as follows:

Case 1 : The unit would have been built in the absence of tax exemptions.

Case 2 : The unit would not have been built in the absence of tax exemptions, and the occupying tenant would have resided elsewhere *within* the city. Multiplier effects of spending excluded.

Case 3a: The unit would not have been built in the absence of tax exemptions, and the occupying tenant would have resided *outside* the city. No additional commercial space generated, and no additional cost of municipal services incurred. Multiplier effects excluded.

Case 3b: Same as 3a, *except* commercial space generated and added cost of municipal services incurred as result of household and commercial expansion. Multiplier effects excluded.

Case 3c: Same as 3b, *except* multiplier effects from construction spending and household spending included.

EXHIBIT 5–2

PER UNIT NET FISCAL IMPACT OF THE 421 PROGRAM UNDER ALTERNATIVE WEIGHTINGS OF ASSUMPTIONS
(Present Discounted Value, 1975-1999)

CASE [1]	NET FISCAL IMPACT [2]	ALTERNATIVE WEIGHTS (PROBABILITIES)										
		a	b	c	d	e	f	g	h	i	j*	k**	l***
1	−$ 9,010	.50	.50	.50	.50	.67	.67	.67	.67	.67	.67	.64	.70
2	16,899	.50	.25	.25	.25	.167	.167	.167	.22	.22	.22	.24	.20
3a	27,341		.25	.25		.167			.11					
3b	14,025			.25	.25		.167			.11		.11	.12	
3c	29,761				.25			.167						.10
Weight Sum	1.00	1.00	1.00	1.00	1.00	1.00	1.00	1.00	1.00	1.00	1.00	1.00	1.00
Per Unit Weighted [3] Net Fiscal Impact (present discounted value)	$3944	$6655	$3226	$7160	$1367	−$853	$1770	$719	−$746	$985	−$28	$49

Notes: *Best estimate of net fiscal impact taking into account multiplier effects and conservative assumptions about ability of program to induce new construction that would not be built in absence of tax exemptions and to attract tenants who would not otherwise reside in city.
**Break-even when multiplier effects are excluded from the analysis.
***Break-even when multiplier effects are included in the analysis.

1. See Exhibit 5-1 for description of cases.
2. See Exhibit 5-1 for calculation of impact for each case.
3. Per unit weighted net fiscal impact is calculated by applying probability weights to impact of each case and summing.

about the most likely distribution of units over the cases are necessary. Our conservative, best estimate is that one-third of the total 421 program units would not have been built without program benefits, and that approximately one-third of the total 421 program units would be occupied by tenants who would not otherwise have resided in the city. This suggests that 67 percent of the units fall into Case 1, 22 percent into Case 2, and 11 percent into Case 3. (We apply the one-third figure for attracting or keeping city residents only to the units that would not otherwise have been built). According to Exhibit 5-2, this indicates a net fiscal impact per unit of $719, ignoring expansion of commercial space and municipal services, and of -746 per unit if there is an expansion of commercial space as well as of municipal services (alternative probabilities h and i of Exhibit 5-2).

If multiplier effects of spending on construction and by induced residents are included in the analysis, the program ends up providing net benefits in terms of taxes: each unit would generate a positive impact of $985 (alternative j). The analysis indicates that the program does not generate positive benefits unless the indirect effects of multiplied spending are taken into account; or, if these are ignored, unless additional city residents do not incur the heavy cost of additional municipal services that we have included. Because of the heavy weight of these costs in our previous calculations, families induced to move to or remain in the city as a result of the program actually create less revenues than residents who would have lived in the city in the absence of program benefits. (If net sales and income tax injection from induced residents, real estate taxes from expanded commercial space, and added costs of municipal services are combined, they total $-2,874$. These are the contributions to the analysis associated with induced residents, excluding the very large multiplier effects.)

How stimulative would the program have to be to at least break even; i.e., provide neither net gains nor losses to the city tax revenues? According to Exhibit 5-2, if 36 percent to 37 percent of the units would not have been built without tax exemption benefits (that is, 63 percent to 64 percent would have been built anyway), then the program will break even without consideration of the multiplier effects but including the long run costs of municipal services (alternative probability k). If multiplier effects are taken into account, then the program would have to be less stimulative to break even—only 30 percent of the units would have to be induced by the program, while 70 percent could have been built even in the absence of tax exemption benefits (alternative probability l). This situation is not terribly different from the degree of stimulation we have assumed as reasonable but conservative—our calculations on the most likely stimulation assumed that 33 percent of the units were induced by the 421 program.

There are many assumptions that have gone into this analysis, but we have tried to be conservative in our assumptions in order not to overstate program benefits to the city. We have assumed a low level of stimulative power (ability to stimulate new construction), low construction-generated municipal revenues and secondary tax impacts from this spending, and a conservative level of retention or attraction of households. The multiplier we have used rests on a very low marginal propensity to consume locally,[67] and we have assumed that marginal costs of common municipal services are equal to the long run average cost of these services.

We therefore conclude that under the most reasonable assumptions about the impact of the 421 program, taking the indirect multiplier effects of spending induced by the program into account, the program actually more than pays its own way. The initial subsidies in the form of property taxes foregone are eventually more than paid back by the stimulation of the city's economy and by the generation of tax revenues from units that would not have been built in the absence of the program (alternative probability j). However, if multiplier effects are ignored, the program appears to impose net costs to the city if the long run expansion of municipal services is taken into account (alternative probability i).

It should be noted that other tax revenues to the city may be forthcoming in addition to those we have included in the calculations if the city incorporates the 421 program into a broader set of programs and policies directed at revitalizing the New York City economy. The joint effect of a set of policies can be expected to exceed the sum of their individual effects.

What Can Be Inferred About J51?

The J51 program—tax abatement and tax exemption to stimulate rehabilitation of the existing housing stock—provides a greater rate of subsidy than the 421 program. While this means that the program is likely to be more stimulative (induce rehabilitation that would not take place in the absence of subsidies), the city tends to bear a higher cost (foregone taxes) relative to the increase in assessed value when compared to the 421 program. On a per dwelling unit basis, however, the level of costs for J51 are likely to be lower because of lower costs of rehabilitation compared to new construction. J51 projects receive a 100 percent exemption on any increase in assessed value for twelve years, plus abatement of up to 90 percent of the certified costs of rehabilitation. 421 projects receive a declining rate of tax exemption (from 100 percent to 20 percent) over a ten year period. In terms of absolute dollars, the subsidies in the 421 program are larger because of the higher increases in assessed value when new construction rather than rehabilitation is undertaken. But relative subsidies are smaller; that is, subsidies relative to the costs of improvements or relative to the increases in assessed value.

We can compare the relationship of tax savings to increases in assessed value for the two programs. The tax effects of the 421 program have been calculated previously. The typical unit receives a total tax saving of $9,010 from the declining tax exemption, assuming a $20,000 increase in assessed value. (This is a hypothetical case.) The tax effects on a typical privately financed major rehabilitation are calculated in Exhibit 5-3. Tax savings from the exemption have a present discounted value of $6,174, while tax savings due to the abatement have a present discounted value of $4,273. The total saving is $10,447 on an increase in assessed value of $7,350. Hence, the ratio of tax savings to increased value is 1.42 for the J51 program and only

0.45 for the 421 program. While it would be more desirable to compare the ratio of tax savings to costs, the absence of data on costs for the 421 program precludes this. We assume, however, that there is a strong relationship between the increase in assessed value and the cost of improvements. The high ratio of savings to value for J51 suggests that this program has greater stimulative power. Indeed, the subsidy is so great that the level of cost savings per unit exceeds that of 421, despite the fact that J51 units have smaller increases in assessed value than do 421 units.[68]

While the J51 program can be expected to be more stimulative in terms of inducing projects to be undertaken, this program may be less likely to attract new residents to the city. J51 buildings are probably both less visible and less attractive to city newcomers than are the larger, newer buildings provided under 421. In particular, advertising of the latter in newspaper ads, an important means by which new tenants are obtained, tends to be on a larger scale. While tenants of both types of programs are likely to be single individuals or couples, and since both programs tend to be skewed toward studio and one bedroom units,[69] the income level of J51 tenants is probably somewhat lower,[70] so that to the extent the program does attract new residents, the generation of tax revenues from their spending streams will be somewhat lower than the 421-project equivalents.

A recent study of J51 indicates that approximately 50 percent of privately financed major rehabilitation projects would have been undertaken in the absence of program benefits.[71] These units impose significant costs in the form of foregone property taxes from abatement and exemption. For the balance of the units that would not otherwise have been built, the program does not start to generate directly any added revenue to the city until the exemptions expire after the twelfth year, and even then these positive tax flows must first cancel out the cost of the abatement before such units reach a break-even point. A small sample of J51 buildings as of 1971-1972 shows certified costs that are eligible for abatement of $5,500 per unit and exemptions of $6,000 per unit.[72] We estimate that this would be

58

EXHIBIT 5–3

PRESENT DISCOUNTED VALUE OF TAXES FOREGONE OR CREATED DUE TO TAX EXEMPTION OR TAX ABATEMENT UNDER J51–PRIVATELY FINANCED MAJOR REHABILITATION

Year	Assessed Value Increase[1]	Tax Rate[2]	Taxes Foregone[2]	$\left(\dfrac{1}{1.08}\right)^t$	Present Value of Taxes Foregone[3]	Present Value of Taxes Abated[4]
1975	$7350	.0819	$602	1.0000	$ 602	$ 561
1976	7350	.0860	632	.9259	585	520
1977	7350	.0903	664	.8573	569	481
1978	7350	.0948	697	.7938	553	445
1979	7350	.0995	731	.7350	538	412
1980	7350	.1045	768	.6806	523	382
1981	7350	.1098	807	.6302	509	353
1982	7350	.1152	847	.5835	494	327
1983	7350	.1210	889	.5403	481	303
1984	7350	.1270	933	.5002	467	281
1985	7350	.1300	956	.4632	443	208
1986	7350	.1300	956	.4289	410	—
					$6,174	$4,273

Taxes per Year on Expired Exemptions:[5]

				Discount Rate[6]	
1987–1999	$7350	.1300	956	3.3897	$3,239[7]

Notes:
1. This is equal to $6,000 × (1.07)³. $6,000 is the actual average exemption per unit on a 15-building sample of privately financed "gut" rehabilitation that entered the program in 1971 and 1972. This figure is increased by 7 percent per year to bring it to a 1975 level.
2. Tax rate is expected to increase at about 5 percent per year for the next ten years and then remain level at $13 per $100 of assessed value for the period 1985-1999.
3. Taxes are discounted back at 8 percent per year. For 1975, t=0.
4. The certified construction costs are estimated to be $6,738. Up to 90 percent of this amount may be abated at a rate of no more than 8.333 percent per year. If the maximum amount is abated in each year, abatements of $561 are taken for a period of 10.8 years. Yearly abatements are discounted back at a rate of 8 percent per year to determine the present discounted value. This is equal to $5,500 × (1.07)³ where $5,500 is the actual average certified cost per unit on a 15-building sample of privately financed "gut" rehabilitations which entered the program in 1971 and 1972.

EXHIBIT 5–3 (Continued)

PRESENT DISCOUNTED VALUE OF TAXES FOREGONE OR CREATED DUE TO TAX EXEMPTION OR TAX ABATEMENT UNDER J51—PRIVATELY FINANCED MAJOR REHABILITATION

5. Alternative Calculation

   1987-1999 Annual Taxes: $.13 \times \$7,350 = \$955.50$

   Present Value 1987 (beginning of term 1987 = end of term 1986)

   $$\$955.50 \frac{(1.+.08)^{13} - 1}{.08(1+.08)^{13}}$$

   $\$955.50(7.904) = \underline{\$7,553}$

   Present Value 1975, where 1975 = year 0:

   $$\$7,553 \frac{1}{(1+.08)^{11}}$$

   $\$7,553(.4289) = \underline{\$3,239}$

6. The discount rate in this instance is the sum of the present worth factors $\left[\left(\dfrac{1}{1.08}\right)^{t}\right]$ from 1987 to 1999.

7. Present value of expired exemptions from 1987 to 1999.

approximately equivalent to certified costs of $6,738 and assessed an annual exemption of $7,350 in the 1975 housing market, using a 7 percent annual rate of inflation. Assuming that one-half of the units would not have been built in the absence of program benefits, the present discounted value of the real estate taxes foregone or generated by exemption and abatement for the period 1975-1999 is equal to −$5,740 per dwelling unit.[73]

Thus we can compare the cost to the city of the typical 421 unit and the typical J51 unit just in terms of the direct property tax costs of abatement and/or exemption. The typical 421 unit has a cost of $475, assuming that one-third of the units would not otherwise have been built (our conservative assumption about the program's stimulative power).[74] The typical J51 unit, on the other hand, has a higher cost per unit of $5,740, even though the increase in assessed value is substantially larger for a unit in the 421 program and even though we have assumed that J51 is more stimulative of improvements that would not otherwise have been made. The high per unit costs of J51 major rehabilitation are a result of the greater rate of exemption and of the added cost of abatement.

In addition, the J51 program is less likely to attract residents who would not otherwise have resided in the city, since the smaller buildings are less visible and less promoted to newcomers than the larger and newer buildings provided under 421. The privately financed major rehabilitations under J51 also tend to have predominantly studio and one-bedroom apartments, which rent for somewhat less than apartments in 421 projects. Hence, while the tenants are likely to be singles or couples, the income levels of the tenants are probably lower; to the extent that the program does attract new or retains present city residents, their spending levels will be lower than those of 421 tenants. Thus, they are likely to generate less added tax revenues to the city than induced residents of the 421 program. Also, the spending on rehabilitation is significantly less than the spending on new construction, which also tends to limit secondary benefits to the city compared with the 421 program.

On the basis of property tax effects due to exemptions or abatement alone, the typical J51 unit is more costly to the city than the typical 421 unit, even though we have assumed that the J51 program is more likely to induce a project to be undertaken that would not have been undertaken in the absence of tax benefits. Moreover, J51 units are less likely to pay back their initial subsidies, since the program is less likely to attract new tenants to the city and since the tenants that it does attract will generate smaller spending streams than tenants of 421 projects.

Conclusions

Housing programs may be viewed within a broader context of stimulation to the economy as a whole. In this light, programs such as 421 and J51 may be seen not simply as subsidies to developers and to middle- or upper-income tenants, but as investments by the city government that may actually repay themselves through the broad stimulative effects of increased assessed values and increased spending on construction and by tenants who would not otherwise reside in the city. These effects depend crucially, however, on how successful the programs are in stimulating projects that would not otherwise have been undertaken.

While the new construction market appears to be in a current state of oversupply, it is believed that this is a temporary phenomenon, certainly encouraged to some extent by the availability of tax subsidies. However, once this surplus is absorbed, developers will once again enter the new construction market, and tax subsidies to facilitate this entry should be considered in the light of their total impact on the city economy.

APPENDIX

NUMBER OF NEW HOUSING UNITS BASED ON BUILDING PERMITS ISSUED BY TYPE OF PROGRAM, NEW YORK CITY, 1963-1973

			Public				Gov't-Assisted Private Middle Income				Public and Gov't-Assisted Private	
Year	Grand Total	Private	Total	State	City	Federal	Total	State	City	Federal	Total	Percent Grand Total
1963	49,898	38,335	5,201	874	—	4,327	6,362	1,401	4,493	468	11,563	23.2
1964	20,596	14,184	1,259	228	—	1,031	5,153	2,771	2,016	366	6,412	31.1
1965	25,715	14,053	3,156	96	—	3,060	8,506	938	6,381	1,187	11,662	45.4
1966	23,142	10,750	1,862	—	440	1,422	10,530	5,962	4,166	402	12,392	53.5
1967	22,172	10,999	3,244	—	573	2,671	7,929	6,035	668	1,224	11,173	50.4
1968	22,062	9,188	1,637	225	—	1,412	11,237	7,421	3,102	714	12,874	58.4
1969	17,031	8,029	1,965	—	—	1,965	7,037	2,168	4,114	755	9,002	52.9
1970	22,365	5,824	2,975	—	—	2,975	13,566	4,938	5,813	2,815	16,541	74.0
1971	32,254	5,654	4,251	1,111	—	3,140	22,349	10,005	8,899	3,445	26,600	82.5
1972	36,061	6,902	3,607	870	—	2,737	25,552	8,148	15,803	1,601	29,159	80.9
1973	22,417	5,883	1,012	—	—	1,012	15,522	3,331	11,108	1,083	16,534	73.8
1974 [1]	15,743	5,604	250	—	—	250	9,889	3,690	6,199	—	10,139	64.4
TOTAL	309,456	135,405	30,419	3,404	1,013	26,002	143,632	56,808	72,762	14,062	174,051	56.2

Note: 1. Preliminary, subject to revision.

Source: New York State Division of Housing and Community Renewal.

Notes

CHAPTER 1

1. Induced construction spending is generated only by those units which would not have been built in the absence of tax exemption benefits.

2. Induced residents are households which would not locate in the city in the absence of program benefits.

CHAPTER 2

3. See George Sternlieb, *The Urban Housing Dilemma* (New York City Housing and Development Administration, 1972).

4. Since the benefits for rehabilitated dwellings are greater under J51 than under 421, it is anticipated that the 421 program will remain predominantly a new construction program.

5. Chapter 1207 of the Laws of New York 1971, most recently amended August 1975 by Chapter 857, Laws of New York 1975.

6. Although rehabilitated units are currently eligible, it is believed that rehabilitation in New York City will be carried out under J51 rather than 421 since the former provides greater subsidies to the owner—a larger exemption over a longer period as well as abatement of rehabilitation costs.

7. Parcels are exempted from any increase in assessed value due to construction during the period of construction.

8. The specified formula for the calculation of initial rents takes into account annual operating and maintenance expenses, projected real property taxes, and total project costs (14 percent of which are allocated annually to project expenses), plus a vacancy and contingency reserve, less a deduction of the annual income on nonresidential uses of the project. Total project costs include land acquisition, site preparation, actual construction or rehabilitation, and off-site requirements. The first two costs are to be certified by an independent public accountant, while the remaining costs are to be determined by the agency in accordance with the amounts which are to be published on January 1 of each year.

9. Telephone conversation with Paul Schultz, Partial Tax Exemption Division, HDA (March 11, 1976). Mr. Schultz also reported that Mitchell-Lama data are currently being analyzed as a basis for determining reasonable costs of operation and maintenance.

10. Jacob Ukeles, et al., *An Assessment of the §421 Limited Tax Exemption Program* (Department of Urban Affairs and Policy Analysis, Center for New York City Affairs, New School for Social Research, April 30, 1975).

11. Telephone conversation with Paul Schultz, Partial Tax Exemption Division, HDA, December 30, 1975.

12. Prior to 1976, only Class A hotels (residential) were eligible. Recent revision of the law has extended eligibility to Class B (transient) hotels.

13. Detailed guidelines were expected to be issued by May 1976.

14. Peter Eilbott and William Kempey, *An Analysis of the J–51–2.5 Tax Abatement and Exemption Program for Stimulating Housing Rehabilitation in New York City* (Department of Economics, Queens College, April 7, 1975).

15. Although painting (other than for removal of lead-based paint hazards), ordinary repairs, and normal replacements were originally ineligible, the recent amendment of the law (1976)

allows these to be included when concurrent with major capital improvements—with some restrictions, however.

16. This program description is based on discussions in Joseph DeSalvo, *An Economic Analysis of New York City's Mitchell-Lama Housing Program* (New York City-Rand Institute, R-610-NYC, June 1971), pp. 1-3.

17. For families of three or less, annual income may not exceed six times annual rent or carrying charges. For families of four or more, income may not exceed seven times annual rent or carrying charges. Surcharges are supposed to be levied on tenants when their incomes exceed the limit.

18. Housing and Development Administration, *City-Assisted Housing Programs, Annual Updating June 1975* (City of New York), pp. A-I, A-II.

19. McKinsey & Company and Housing and Development Administration, *Analysis of Mitchell-Lama Projects in Occupancy* (1973).

20. When a tenant's income exceeds the program limit, a surcharge is supposed to be levied (see note 17).

21. Division of Housing and Community Renewal, *Statistical Summary of Programs* (State of New York, March 31, 1975), p. 65.

22. Telephone conversation with Arthur Shulman, Associate Economist, Division of Housing and Community Renewal, State of New York, December 16, 1975.

23. The Finance Administration lists as 588 the number of tax exemptions under the 421 program; however, this includes one condominium project of approximately 400 units in which each unit receives an individual exemption (telephone conversation with Joseph Aronson, Senior Statistician, Department of Real Property Assessment, Finance Administration, City of New York, January 13, 1976).

24. The 1974-75 real property tax rate was $7.35 per $100 of assessed value. Applying this rate to the dollar value of exemptions, $884 million, yields foregone taxes of $65 million.

CHAPTER 3

25. The Mitchell-Lama law states its purpose as correcting emergency conditions resulting from an inadequate supply of safe and sanitary housing for low-income and aged families. However, the program has been generally accepted as a means of benefiting middle-income families, in particular those with children (DeSalvo, p. 2).

26. While economic theory suggests that the goal of income redistribution is best served through cash transfers rather than subsidies to particular markets, social concern with the external effects of housing and with paternalistic specification of what consumers should consume has made the housing market a major mechanism by which income is redistributed. Moreover, it is probably easier for the city to forego property taxes in order to provide subsidies rather than to appropriate funds explicitly either for unrestricted cash subsidies or for cash subsidies restricted to the housing market.

27. Given the high costs of housing rehabilitation and construction as well as the smaller secondary tax effects associated with lower-income households, it would be difficult to argue that a program restricted to lower-income households would similarly pay for itself. However, if the city incurs net costs for such a program, these costs could then be justified as desirable income redistribution. Unfortunately, the current realities of New York City's finances have severely restricted its ability to carry out this function.

28. This descriptive model is not restricted to evaluating the 421 program; thus, the discussion is couched within the context of new construction and rehabilitation.

29. In support of this claim is the fact that many projects receiving J51 subsidies filed for benefits quite a few years after rehabilitation had been completed. While an owner may file for benefits only upon completion of rehabilitation, the current law allows for up to a three-year delay in applying; an earlier version of the law allowed for much longer delays for housing rehabilitated between 1955 and 1970 (Eilbott and Kempey, p. 17).

While owners usually file for 421 benefits prior to initiation of construction, a number of projects have been admitted to the program after construction was completed (telephone conversation with Paul Schultz, Partial Tax Exemption Section, Housing and Development Administration, City of New York, December 30, 1975).

30. Both owners and tenants of rental properties in the programs benefit from abatement or exemption if the owner passes on a portion of his cost savings to the tenants in the form of lower rents. Under 421, initial rents are supposed to be set 15 percent below comparable market rents. Under J51, it is administrative policy that initial rents be rolled back by an amount equal to two-thirds of the first year's abatement. (J51 and 421 projects are initially subject to either rent control or rent stabilization. Vacancy decontrol in these projects would have reduced or eliminated benefits to tenants. Administrative delays in J51 rollbacks have also reduced tenant benefits.) Mitchell-Lama units are regulated so that the limited-profit sponsor receives a 6 percent return on equity.

31. Eilbott and Kempey, pp. 7-8. Data on rent changes before and after rehabilitation were indicative of a change in tenantry from lower-income to higher-income households.

32. In a recent study of the J51 program, it was estimated that 40 percent to 60 percent of the privately financed major rehabilitation would have been undertaken in the absence of subsidy. This conclusion was based on the fact that 60 percent of the projects had rates of return in excess of the rate of return allowed under the Maximum Base Rent Program (8.5 percent), while 40 percent of the buildings had rates of return in excess of a higher estimate of an acceptable market rate of return. This higher estimate of 12.6 percent on total investment prior to depreciation was the rate for buildings in the J51 program which had applied for benefits only after substantial time lags (Eilbott and Kempey, p. 42). This suggests that, using the former criterion, 60 percent of the projects would have been undertaken in the absence of subsidy, and using the latter criterion, 40 percent would have been undertaken in the absence of subsidy.

33. Just as some units would have been built in the absence of program benefits, some tenants would have been induced to reside in the city or move to the city in the absence of program benefits. Only inward migration induced by the subsidies (that migration which would not have taken place without subsidies) represents a net gain to the city.

34. While a small number of additional households can be accommodated within the existing commercial space and existing infrastructure and levels of public services, long run expansion of public and private facilities does reflect the impact of each marginal household.

35. The relatively high city sales tax suggests that builders attempt to minimize purchases of supplies within the city.

36. Housing that filters down to other tenants may be located either within the city or elsewhere, depending upon the previous residence of tenants living in housing receiving exemptions or abatements.

37. The original 421 program restricted eligible projects to vacant land or underutilized sites, but provided no precise definition of underutilization. In 1975, the law was revised so that in the case of displacement of tenants from an existing multiple dwelling of at least twenty units, the newly constructed structure must contain at least five units for every previously occupied unit. Approximately 14 percent of the units in the 421 program through 1974 were on sites in which the replacement ratio of new to demolished units was less than five. (Ukeles et al., p. 14).

38. The city does bear the administrative costs of the programs, but recent changes in the J51 and 421 programs provide for application fees which will at least partially offset administrative costs.

39. While Mitchell-Lama projects in "mid-rent" neighborhoods seemed to have an impact on the value of adjacent parcels, projects in both "high-rent" and "low-rent" neighborhoods seemed to have no significant impact (DeSalvo, p. 32).

40. "Long run" is used in the sense that expansion of public and private facilities occurs.

41. It is not known what fraction of 421 housing would have been built in the absence of program benefits. However, a recent study of the J51 tax exemption-tax abatement program for rehabilitation of existing structures found that, at most, 60 percent of privately financed major rehabilitation projects would not have been undertaken without program benefits—using a conservative estimate of free-market rates of return on total investment as a benchmark. Forty percent of projects had rates of return in excess of the rate on a subset of buildings which did not apply for benefits until several years after the completion of rehabilitation. The median rate of return for buildings in this subgroup was 12.6 percent on total investment before depreciation (Eilbott and Kempey, p. 38). Because the rate of subsidy is smaller under 421, the 421 program would be less stimulative to investment; that is, less likely to induce investment that would not have been undertaken without tax exemption benefits. (Under 421, there is a ten year period of declining tax exemption on the increased assessed value. Under J51, the increase in assessed value due to rehabilitation is fully exempt for a period of twelve years, in addition to which property taxes are abated for a period of not less than nine years nor more than twenty years, with annual abatement not to exceed 90 percent of the certified reasonable cost of rehabilitation.) Not only is the rate of subsidy lower under 421, but it is reasonable to assume that a higher rate of return would be required to induce new construction rather than rehabilitation of existing housing.

CHAPTER 4

42. Induced construction spending is generated only by those units that would not have been built in the absence of tax exemption benefits.

43. Induced residents are households that would not locate in the city in the absence of program benefits.

44. Both the increases in tax rate and the city's cost of money are clearly open to question. It may be hoped, however, that

stabilization of the tax rate as a result of capping the revenue expenditures squeeze would also yield an offset of municipal borrowing costs.

45. The $14,000 figure is calculated from data in Ukeles et al., p. 32.

46. Induced construction spending is generated only by those units which would *not* have been built in the absence of tax exemption benefits.

47. Estimated construction cost per unit for units then under construction in the New York City Mitchell-Lama program in 1975 was approximately $41,000. The typical unit under construction contained 4.4 rooms; therefore, per room cost is approximately $9,400 (Division of Housing and Community Renewal, *Statistical Summary of Programs,* New York State, March 31, 1975, p. 65). Using this per unit figure we get a cost of $28,000 for a three-room unit. However, this probably understates the cost since the cost per room declines as the number of rooms per unit increases because of the fixed costs of bathrooms and kitchens. Some higher costs would also be expected because 421 units are somewhat more luxurious than Mitchell-Lama units, and because they tend to be weighted toward Manhattan and higher-rise construction. Hence, even our $30,000 per unit estimate is conservative.

48. Multiplier effects result from the fact that any initial injection of spending goes into the pockets of households and firms and some portion is respent. This cycle repeats itself, although each round is smaller and smaller because of leakages into savings, taxes, or spending outside the local economy.

49. According to a 1969 study by McKinsey & Company, in new construction 40 percent of construction costs goes to labor, 45 percent to materials, and the remaining 15 percent to overhead and profit components of construction costs. (McKinsey & Company, *Defining Potential City Initiatives in the Stimulation of Private New Residential Construction,* New York, October 1, 1969.)

50. Induced construction spending is generated only by those units which would *not* have been built in the absence of tax exemption benefits.

51. The 0.4 marginal propensity to consume locally is our estimate after taking account of leakages into savings of households and firms, leakages from the spending stream through various forms of taxation, and spending outside the local economy. The estimate is very conservative.

52. This 8 percent figure is based on analysis of the household budget presented in Exhibit 4–4. Sales and income taxes amount to somewhat less than 2 percent of the household income. While property taxes are not fully paid for this family because of the tax exemption, if taxes equaling approximately 25 percent of rent were paid, then the tax contribution would rise to 8 percent of income.

53. Induced residents are households induced to move into the city by the program or induced not to leave the city by the program. Only such households living in units that would not have been built in the absence of program benefits generate benefits or costs that are a part of the program impact.

54. Vacation transportation is included in the miscellaneous taxable item. If airfare is purchased within the city for a vacation outside the city, then the city sales tax is paid.

55. It is interesting to note that the Internal Revenue Service allows for a deduction of exactly $211 in sales taxes paid to the city for a two-person household with adjusted gross income of $25,000 (*1975 Federal Income Tax Forms*, p. 29). This is the calculation for New York State sales taxes, but the allowance for the city sales tax would correspond exactly, since city and state sales taxes are each 4 percent.

56. While this same family is not likely to remain in the unit or have similar expenditure patterns over twenty-five years, it is assumed that a similar family will take occupancy and be in the same life cycle stage that the original family was in when it took occupancy. This change in tenantry should repeat itself over the economic life of the dwelling unit.

57. Induced residents are households induced either to move into or to stay in the city because of the program.

58. This is equal to income ($25,000) less sales taxes to the city and state for expenditures in the city ($423), less expenditures outside the city ($540 for food and miscellaneous taxable

items, $60 for gasoline), less spending which would have taken place even if the household did not live within the city ($856 = .15 × $5,710), less other gasoline taxes (500 gallons × $.12 = $60), less savings ($1,990), less federal, state, and city income taxes ($6,770). This leaves a net injection of local spending, exclusive of all taxes, of $14,301.

59. We assume that eight cents on the dollar ends up in sales, income, or property taxes. This is based on an analysis of the estimated household budget in Exhibit 4–4. Sales and income taxes amount to somewhat less than 2 percent of income. If property taxes were fully paid, the figures would rise to 8 percent.

60. Changes in sales, income, and property tax rates are ignored over the period so that multiplier effects on taxes will be understated.

61. "Long run" refers to a time at which the firm will be able to expand capacity. It is not so much a time dimension as a measure of the firm's flexibility to vary production. If expansion of space coincides with expansion of residential space, then the long run begins when the program begins.

62. Transportation expenditures are excluded from the analysis.

63. Even if this additional retail volume does not generate additional space to be taxed, its results would, in the long run, be equivalent in reinforcing the economic viability and value of existing facilities.

64. This is consistent with our assumptions about property taxes as discussed in the previous section on property taxes foregone or created by exemptions.

65. $$\$2368 = \sum_{t=0}^{9} \$153 \left(\frac{1.05}{1.08}\right)^t + \sum_{t=10}^{24} \$153 \frac{(1.05)^9}{(1.08)^t}$$
$$= \quad \$1352 \quad + \quad \$1016$$

Even though spending by the household is expected to increase 6 percent per year, we do not assume that this will result in an expansion of commercial space beyond the initial adjustment.

CHAPTER 5

66. We have used average expenditures on common municipal services per capita as an indicator of marginal cost on the assumption that long run costs are constant in the relevant range. Common municipal services include all items in the city budget except hospitals, education and welfare outlays, and debt service payments. See Exhibit 4–12, and George Sternlieb et al., *Housing Development and Municipal Costs* (Rutgers University, Center for Urban Policy Research, 1973).

67. We assume a 0.4 marginal propensity to consume locally, yielding a multiplier of 1.67. Multipliers for various sectors of the Portsmouth, New Hampshire economy range from 1.4 to 1.8, but such a city would have substantial leakage into imports compared with New York (Werner C. Hirsch, *Urban Economic Analysis*, New York: McGraw-Hill, 1973, p. 246).

68. J51 calculations are based on a sample of fifteen privately financed major rehabilitation projects that entered the J51 program in 1971 and 1972. The data were provided by Peter Eilbott of Queens College. 1971-72 figures have been updated for comparability with our 1975 analysis of 421.

69. A recent study of the 421 program found that 60 percent of all 421 program units were one-bedroom units or studios, and 78 percent of Manhattan units were in this range (Ukeles et al., p. 29). A study of the J51 program reports that the great bulk of rehabilitated apartments were studios and one-bedroom units (Eilbott and Kempey, p. 8).

70. Rents tend to be higher in 421 program units, so it may be concluded that their tenants tend to have higher incomes. The average rent per unit in 247 units in fifteen buildings in the J51 program in 1971-72 was $229 (data provided by Peter Eilbott, Queens College). Average rent per room for 421 program units built between 1971 and 1975 was $126, suggesting that a one-bedroom unit would rent for approximately $400-$450 (Ukeles, p. 31). Although the data are for different years, the difference in rents is substantial enough to conclude that 421 program tenants must have higher incomes than J51 pro-

gram tenants, assuming that wide variations in rent-income ratios do not exist.

71. Eilbott and Kempey, pp. 7–8.

72. This is a sample of fifteen buildings containing 247 units which entered the J51 program in 1971 and 1972. The raw data were provided by Peter Eilbott, Queens College.

73. For each unit that would have been built without program benefits, the cost of foregone taxes is equal to the sum of tax abatements plus the value of tax savings from the exemptions. The present discounted value of abatements for the 10.8 year period beginning in 1975 is equal to $4,273. Tax savings from the exemption have a present discounted value of $6,174 for the twelve year period beginning in 1975. (The 10.8 year period for the abatement is equal to .90/.08333, the maximum rate of abatement divided by the annual maximum rate.) Hence each unit which would have been built in the absence of program benefits generates a total tax cost of $10,447. For each unit that would not have been built in the absence of program benefits, the city foregoes the abated taxes of $4,273, but the cost of the exemptions is zero because the building would not have been improved, and there is a gain on expired exemptions of $3,239 from 1987 to 1999 that it would not otherwise have received. Hence, such a unit would actually generate negative impact of $-$1,034. (Expired exemptions are irrelevant to units that would otherwise have been built since the city would have received these tax revenues anyway.) Weighting under the assumption that one-half of the units would have been built and one-half would not, the net impact per unit with respect to the effects of the abatement and exemption is equal to $-$5,740; that is, the city incurs a net cost of $5,740 per unit (i.e., 0.5 of $10,447 + 0.5 of $-$1,034).

74. $-$480 = 2/3 × ($-$9,010) + 1/3 ($16,596) where $9,010 represents taxes foregone if a unit would have been built anyway and $16,596 represent taxes created if a unit would not have been built. These are present discounted values including the period of expired exemptions (1987-1999).